ReWiring the Corporate Brain

Up My Mother's Flagpole (a humorous autobiography)

Israel: The Land and Its People

Through the Time Barrier

The Quantum Self

The Quantum Society (co-author, Ian Marshall)

Who's Afraid of Schrödinger's Cat? (co-author, Ian Marshall)

ReWiring the Corporate Brain

Using the
New Science
to Rethink
How We
Structure
and Lead
Organizations

DANAH ZOHAR

Berrett-Koehler Publishers, Inc.
San Francisco

Berrett-Koehler Publishers, Inc.
450 Sansome Street, Suite 1200
San Francisco, CA 94111-3320
Tel: (415) 288-0260 Fax: (415) 362-2512

Ordering Information

Individual sales. Berrett-Koehler publications are available through most bookstores. They can also be ordered direct from Berrett-Koehler at the address above.

Quantity sales. Special discounts are available on quantity purchases by corporations, associations, and others. For details, contact the "Special Sales Department" at the Berrett-Koehler address above.

Orders for college textbook/course adoption use. Please contact Berrett-Koehler Publishers at the address above.

Orders by U.S. trade bookstores and wholesalers. Please contact Publishers Group West, 4065 Hollis Street, Box 8843, Emeryville, CA 94662. Tel: (510) 658–3453; 1-800-788-3123. Fax: (510) 658-1834.

Printed in the United States of America

Printed on acid-free and recycled paper that is composed of 85% recovered fiber, including 15% postconsumer waste.

Library of Congress Cataloging-in-Publication Data

Zohar, Danah, 1945–
   Rewiring the corporate brain: using the new science to rethink how we structure and lead organizations / by Danah Zohar.
      p. cm.
   Includes bibliographical references and index.
   ISBN 1-57675-022-1 (alk. paper)
   1. Industrial organization—Psychological aspects. 2. Industrial management—Psychological aspects. 3. Leadership. I. Title.
HD2326.Z64   1997
658.4′063—dc21   97-33499
                                                           CIP

First Edition
00 99 98 97   10 9 8 7 6 5 4 3 2 1

Copyediting: Hilary Powers
Proofreading: Mary Lou Sumberg
Interior design and production: Joel Friedlander Publishing Services
Indexing: Evergreen Valley Indexing
Jacket: Cassandra Chu

For Sven Atterhed, with thanks.

Most transformation programs satisfy themselves with shifting the same old furniture about in the same old room. Some seek to throw some of the furniture away. But real transformation requires that we redesign the room itself. Perhaps even blow up the old room. It requires that we change the thinking behind our thinking—literally, that we learn to rewire our corporate brains.

—Danah Zohar

Contents

Foreword

S cience, particularly the new science of the twentieth century, has always strongly affected my thinking. Ideas I have come across and internalized from quantum mechanics and chaos theory reflect changes in the way I manage. But it has been difficult for me to describe this symbiotic relationship between business and science.

The enjoyment of this, the latest of Danah Zohar's insightful books, is in her ability to clarify for those who don't know (and even for some who say they do) the thinking behind the new sciences. She helps to show how this powerful new mind-set allows science to comprehend the universe in a more exciting way. She explains how businesspeople can use it to conceive patterns that exist in the more complex situations that the new pace, scale, and advanced technologies have developed within our companies.

In my business life, people in positions of authority who are able to tell me exactly what they do and how they do it always impress me at first. They seem so in control. However, subsequently, I often find that they don't actually do what they do very well. Their certainty is an illusion, and perhaps a damaging one. As Danah Zohar points out in this book, there may be a necessary interplay between uncertainty and a kind of creativity in what we do. Heisenberg's famous principle can affect us all, even in daily life and business.

Scientists, when trying to explain reality, are frustrated by our human intelligence and the limits of vocabulary and mathematical terms. Artists strive to capture the essence of the universe and enable us to experience it with our emotions. They use the language of form, color, shape, or performance. Scientists and artists, when they are in dialogue, stimulate each other to attain new insights.

Those of us who are dealing with the management of vibrant businesses are also trying to clarify and simplify complex dynamics by seeing patterns that can be understood, communicated, and controlled. We tend to say we like to keep things simple, but actually leadership at our level is both an art and a science. In some important sense, it is beyond control, beyond the limits of the known and the sayable.

What amazes me is how reluctant people in business are to admit that science fascinates them. I have always enjoyed reading science, perhaps because maths and biology were the only subjects I didn't fail at school. Yet my own passion has sometimes left me feeling out of place in business circles. While many of my colleagues are comfortable talking socially about art, music, and the theater, about sport, politics, and of course trade, they seem shy about science. If I feel enthusiastic about a book on Darwinism or consciousness, I feel colleagues may be willing to talk about it privately, but would rather I didn't bring it up at the dinner table. There seem to be quite a few closet scientists in business.

Yet at Marks & Spencer, we have always made use of science in almost everything we do. Science was a force in the company long before my arrival. Simon Marks and Israel Sieff were lifelong friends of Chaim Weizmann, the British chemist who became the first president of Israel. He taught them the relevance of scientific theory to business. He also involved them in the politics of the emerging nation and showed how, in addition to the part science plays in war, it can also work for peace.

In the late 1970s, I was Lord Sieff's personal assistant when he was chairman of Marks & Spencer. He was trying to help Egypt and Israel see the value of peace. We were involved in making connections through commercial and cultural routes. He used to say, "Where politics, diplomacy, or military means often fail, science, art, and commerce can cross international borders, ignore ethnic boundaries, and increase understanding, helping people who would normally fight to become friends."

Having spent most of the 1960s selling on street markets in Wales, I was surprised to find myself in the late 1980s being put in positions of authority and responsibility that I hadn't planned for at all. I looked for sources of knowledge and wisdom to help me recognize patterns and processes within social organizations. I hoped these could provide me with some insight into how to manage them.

Unlike those managers with certainty to whom I referred earlier, I have never known exactly how I do what I do. I do know that the people and the systems around me are of high quality and are effective. I would like to know more about this interaction between leader, people, and systems in complex organizations.

I do not find that I learn new methods from business school courses and conventional books on management. What I do enjoy is when an article or a lecture—or a book like *Rewiring the Corporate Brain*—clarifies a process that we in business use instinctively. Such things can be helpful by lending our instinctive processes a terminology, by putting them into context and bringing them to the front of consciousness. At that point, it becomes possible to get a clearer picture of what we have been doing and then develop the natural process into a technique that can be used effectively when appropriate.

Scientists do this all the time—observing processes, defining them within an overall cohesive system, and proving that, when observed again, the outcome is predictable. Multinational corporations are complex organizations comprising thousands of individuals of varying cultures and ethnic heritages. The activities of the company affect those individuals, the society in which they trade, and the world environment. The governance of these communities must be cognizant of the same issues as the leadership of any town, state, or even nation-state. Perhaps they should be put under the microscope, as they are in *Rewiring the Corporate Brain*. By doing so, Danah Zohar puts our business processes and interactions and leadership styles within a larger scientific framework.

Any organization can be understood in terms of its beginnings and growth. Marks & Spencer, for example, started as a one-man street peddler in 1884, grew to become a U.K. store chain then an international retailer, and is evolving into a global corporation. The company has lived for over a hundred years. It is an organism with its own "brain," its own identity, personality, and philosophy: enlightened self-interest.

Marks & Spencer has partners who act as an extended family of suppliers. The company acts as if it has eyes and ears and seems to have its own consciousness. It responds to external stimuli—both with immediate reflexes and with more considered strategies. It communicates with the outside world. Its instinct for survival and drive for more knowledge and new experiences are almost palpable. I invited Danah Zohar into the company to observe this. I am now fascinated to see her describe our processes within the conceptual framework of the new science. She has articulated what is certainly one of our basic company paradigms.

Science is not the only paradigm we use at Marks & Spencer to think things through. Ethics and philosophy, art and political history have also provided valuable insights. What fascinates me more than any other issue is the dynamics of the development of organizations. They appear to be self-regulating, learning societies. Given the right initial state, they develop their own laws or principles that govern survival and growth. I take great pleasure in understanding these principles, what brought them into being, and how they become policy. People assume that as an innovator, I break rules. I don't. I relish rules. I just like rewriting them.

The dynamics of developing organizations cannot be controlled by military, mechanical, or monetary management. Such tools are inadequate to cope with the increased complexity of today's business. A retailer trading in thirty or forty countries in the Americas, Europe, and Asia will be dealing longitudinally in all the world's time zones and latitudinally in both hemispheres. Open twenty-four hours a day with summer, winter, spring, and autumn happening somewhere simultaneously, the company must always be awake. So how do we control the organization now that it is so broadly spread out and multidimensional?

Obviously, you don't have to be a quantum physicist to run a successful global business. Nevertheless, scientific theory has influence on our everyday thought processes. Leaders of organizations generally gain their scientific insight secondhand, as theories seep their way into society after decades of use. We all have an image of Bohr's indestructible atoms with particles like solar systems, of Newton's mechanical action-and-reaction, of Darwin's survival of the fittest.

The ways we hold many of these concepts in our imaginations are now outdated. Just as they no longer explain the universe scientifically, they are inadequate to help conceive of the complex dynamics of business.

I came across Danah Zohar when I read her first best-selling book on consciousness and quantum physics, *The Quantum Self.* I found it accessible, clear, and informative. Danah had made me—and I am sure many of her readers—believe we were experts, too. I even had the audacity to write her and suggest that she come for lunch. I felt that I, with a perhaps different perspective from a scientist, could demonstrate to her phenomena within our organization that could possibly be described as "quantum."

Danah was patient and humored me for a while, but by the time we were on pudding, she told me quite subtly to stick to selling and leave science to the scientists. However, she did admit that listening to how businesspeople perceived and resolved issues would lead her to reconsider in some ways her thinking about scientific problems. She also suggested that her scientific method could help me approach business from a different angle.

In the next few years, we met several times and Danah visited Marks & Spencer directors' meetings to observe how we work. She used these conversations and visits to wed her understanding of processes in the new science to our own management processes. Now she has written about this in *Rewiring the Corporate Brain.*

Danah's insights articulate what we have always done naturally. The connections she makes between quantum physics and the corporation provide an explanation, or a conceptual framework, for a management style such as mine, hitherto seen to be chaotic.

I believe that what we businesspeople need to understand about twentieth-century science is not technical. It is conceptual. Science is continually bringing forth new technologies, and business will always absorb these naturally through product innovation and applied systems. But science also brings forth new thinking. In the past few decades, science has discovered new conceptual insights that might have application to our organizations and how we lead them. If we nonscientists are helped in our attempts at understanding, we might be able to discern and foresee patterns unfolding in the process of our trade that can be predicted and controlled.

Rewiring the Corporate Brain helps to clarify the relevance of new scientific concepts to business. Some of the examples that impressed me most in the book are:

• *How the new science of consciousness studies the human mind.* We are awake for sixteen hours and yet our brain is monitoring and controlling our twenty-four-hour complex body. Our intelligence seems to make sense of a multidimensional universe to allow individuals to function efficiently. The collective mind of our company seems to work in the same way. Danah's description of the new reworking of theories about the relationship between mind and brain led me to believe that the better we can connect the mind of our company with its extremities, the healthier our company will be.

• *How communication happens by other than linear command.* Things happen in our business in Hong Kong and Aberdeen at exactly the same time. The quantum simultaneity, or nonlocality, that Danah describes so well is as much a fascination for global business as it is for physicists. It gives us a concrete model of simultaneity, cooperation, and synchronicity.

• *How the "wave-particle duality" of quantum physics applies to business situations.* Commercial trends and examples of waves are to a certain extent predictable. But at the "atomic" level, single events and the actions of individual customers are unpredictable particles.

• *How consciousness, simultaneity, evolution, and the rewiring of the brain are all intriguing concepts relating as much to business as to any other facet of the universe.*

Scientists, in their search for a unified theory revel in the diversity of the fields in which they work. Artists live for the high they attain in creating and performing new works. Businesspeople strive to create centers of excellence. We too should be liberated by the insight that there is no one right answer. We should come out of the closet, and, like scientists and artists, enjoy our divine discontent. We should be thrilled by the variety of patterns and paradigms emanating from the brilliant minds who have given us science. As a businessman, I believe many colleagues could benefit from this latest of Danah Zohar's contributions to explaining the relevance of the new science to wider facets of society.

—Lord Andrew Stone,
Joint Managing Director,
Marks & Spencer plc
London, England

Preface

The notion that individual organizations have "brains" functioning much like those of individual human beings was first put to me in a letter from Andrew Stone six years ago. Stone was then one of the thirteen directors of Britain's global retailing giant, Marks & Spencer. I had just published a book on the mind and its brain *(The Quantum Self)*, and he felt that some ideas from the book applied to trends he had noticed in his organization.

By suggesting that Marks & Spencer had a brain of its own, Stone meant that he saw self-organizing and self-reinforcing patterns of behavior in his company that seemed to function almost as though independent of the individuals who managed it. As he wrote to me: "My work is in a building that houses three thousand people who are essentially the individual 'particles' of the 'brain' of an organization that consists of sixty thousand people worldwide. The organization is seen to have an identity (it has been in existence for over a hundred years), it has a mind and a will and an intelligence that exist in the absence of these people (when the office is shut), but it is dependent on the interaction of the individuals from which it is constituted."

Today, Andrew Stone is joint managing director of Marks & Spencer. He is now among a still small but significant number of the world's top CEOs who say openly that much of their leadership style is strongly influenced by images and ideas they have encountered from the new science of the twentieth century. Concepts from physics and biology like quantum uncertainty and holism or self-organization "at the edge of chaos," notions that there can be a useful "fuzzy logic" or "adaptive evolution," and discoveries from cognitive science and neurobiology that the human brain has an infinite capacity to grow new neural connections (to rewire itself) all seem to have tantalizing relevance to the structure and leadership of the organizations they run. In Stone's case, he attributes his fascination with quantum physics and brain science to a hope that these can shed more light on how the "brain" of Marks & Spencer works "so I can help it become more efficient."

This book is about brains, both human and organizational, about how they are structured and the kinds of thinking processes generated by different structures. More important, it is about the transformation or rewiring of these brains, about the restructuring processes the human brain uses to readapt itself to new environments and how these point the way toward really fundamental organizational transformation.

It is also a book about science, about the way that old, Newtonian scientific thinking limits and distorts management thinking in an age of growing complexity and rapid change, and how new scientific thinking can show us a better way. The concepts, categories, images, and metaphors found in twentieth-century science—in quantum physics and in chaos and complexity science—represent a revolution in human thinking. "Quantum thinking" issues from a different part of the brain than Newtonian thinking. Learning to *do* quantum thinking is in itself an effective tool for rewiring the brain. Combined with the dialogue technique as a practical application of quantum thinking, it is the main tool I have to offer in this book for rewiring the corporate brain.

By training, I am a physicist and philosopher. I first discovered quantum physics when I was thirteen years old and it was to change my life forever. The quantum world seemed magical, alive, marvelously unpredictable and filled with wonderful surprise. I immersed myself in its language and imagery, conducted mad-scientist experiments with atom smashers and cloud chambers in my bedroom, and used quantum metaphors to address those "big questions" that adolescents ask.

I won a scholarship to study physics at MIT when I was eighteen. Within three months of my arrival, I realized it wasn't physics itself that interested me so much as the *philosophy* of physics—how physics in particular, but the newest science in general, gives us a new way to think about wider issues in our lives. I took a double degree in physics and philosophy at MIT, and then went on to Harvard Graduate School to do a rich mix of postgraduate work in philosophy, psychology, theology, and law. The rest of my life has been spent thinking and writing about how the new science—especially quantum physics—gives us a new way to think (and a correspondingly new way to *act*) in many aspects of our lives.

After I had published my two books, *The Quantum Self* and *The Quantum Society,* I began getting invitations to lecture in the corporate world. Managers wanted to know how the new science might be applied to the need for new thinking about business. As the last five years have passed, I have come to spend the bulk of my time working with senior executives in large companies around the world.

One of the first senior managers from whom I heard in those early days was Andrew Stone at Marks & Spencer. I was immediately impressed by what he told me about his company, but even more so by Stone's own management style and by his ability to articulate much of what he was doing in terms of the new science. Stone gave me access to the company and many opportunities to observe him at work. In consequence, many of the examples of quantum corporate thinking offered in this book are from Marks & Spencer.

Other companies where I have worked and have since had opportunity to observe are too numerous to mention. But the men and women in each of them have taught me a great deal along the way, and I am grateful to them. I am particularly grateful for the openness and honesty with which senior corporate people have shared their problems, their frustrations, and their visions of a better way. Many examples of comments and observations they have offered are included in the book. I particularly enjoyed returning to Volvo Car Corporation in Sweden after a gap of almost two years and witnessing the quantum changes the company has made to its car-making teams. This, too, is discussed later in the book.

There are individuals who have contributed a great deal in one way or another to the making of this book. With Bill Isaacs at MIT, I have had the opportunity to share rich insights about the theory and practice of dialogue. Joe Jaworski from the United States and S.K. Chakraborty of Calcutta's Indian Institute of Management have contributed their powerful personal examples of servant leadership. Sven Atterhed of the Foresight Group in Sweden has been a constant friend and colleague, making bridges with many Scandinavian companies. R.S. Moorthy at Motorola has been great fun to work with and has given me many valuable insights, some of which are developed in the book. My colleagues at Peter Chadwick Ltd. have provided both a rich model of what a consultancy group might be and an arena in which I have been able to spread my own wings further. I am particularly glad to be developing the Peter Chadwick Leadership Institute with Peter Isaac. And my husband, Ian Marshall, has, as always, contributed a great many ideas to the book, particularly his work on the three kinds of thinking.

I very much hope that readers of this book will enjoy reading it as much as I have enjoyed writing it, and that some at least will have learned to share the passion that I feel for the new science and the gift of its new thinking.

—Danah Zohar
Oxford, England
August, 1997

Introduction:
The Transformation Lie

The CEO of a global company for which I have worked recently kicked off his corporation's new "senior leadership transformation program." He spoke openly and frankly, "from the heart," to the top 150 in his worldwide management team. He told them the story of his personal journey toward becoming a broader person, "a person who is not afraid of his own or others' feelings." He urged his colleagues to become more sensitive human beings, to pay greater heed to vision and value, to encourage greater openness and experiment in those whom they lead.

"And why are we doing this?" he asked, in that rah-rah football coach style CEOs use in motivational speeches. "We are doing it so we can beat the hell out of the competition!" It was not a joke, and nobody laughed. This leader saw no contradiction between his visionary words and the goal that motivated them.

Transformation is the great obsession of our fearful and dissatisfied change-conscious culture. Millions (if not billions) are spent each year by corporations, small businesses, and health and education authorities on large-scale transformation programs. Privately, many millions of individuals spend millions of dollars seeking personal transformation at the hands of psychotherapists, analysts, stress managers, gurus, and religious sects. Yet scarcely anyone knows what real transformation entails, and few would want it if they did.

I think that transformation is the great lie of the corporate world. A large part of the lie is the misuse and abuse of language—the distortion of words like transformation, restructuring, recontextualizing, vision and value, openness, from the heart, and change itself. Many corporate transformation programs are initiated by leaders who want greater control over their markets and employees. They see them as a step up in the battle against their competitors. These men got to the top following the rules of

1

the only game they know. Most are terrified of change. The programs themselves are often run by consultant witch doctors who charge high fees to create the illusion of real action. They wave magical flip charts and speak the latest transformation doublespeak, but their purpose is to ensure that nobody becomes too uncomfortable, that nothing fundamental really changes. Even the *illusion* of change must be delivered quickly, in quantifiable data, to impatient clients.

The most innovative of the so-called corporate change processes talk about "restructuring" and "reengineering." Both are merely surface solutions. They shift the furniture about in the room (the corporation), sometimes they throw some of the furniture away, but they keep the same old room. They have no more lasting consequence than political revolutions that put a new party in power but maintain all the old structures. Society itself doesn't change. Nor does the reengineered corporation. All that remains is the trauma and pollution of human waste in the wake of downsized organizations. And the dissatisfaction of disgruntled customers whose services have been vastly cut, as with the British banks that have closed local branches in the name of centralization and efficiency. Real change, fundamental transformation, requires that we change the underlying patterns of thought and emotion that created the old structures in the first place. It means that we have to redesign the room. Stronger still, it may mean that we have to tear the old room apart and start anew.

Transformation requires change linked to meaning, that is, that those who would make changes *understand* what is wrong and why it needs changing. Change and meaning are the two themes that come up again and again in my own work with companies, though they are seldom linked. They are also the two dominant themes troubling people in the wider culture.

How do we adjust to, cope with, learn to thrive on the constant and rapid changes in our personal and business lives? How do we learn to shift our thinking deeply enough and quickly enough—learn to think on our feet? And how, in our efficiency-dominated, results-oriented business lives do we find a bridge to the more personal and deeper layers of meaning and relationship that make both life and work worthwhile? Real change must issue from those deep levels of our human being where we are in touch with meaning and value. It is not something we can do in order to "beat the hell out of the competition."

Such deep transformation is not easy. It often hurts and it is usually terribly slow. It requires that people who experience it feel uncomfortable, even perhaps that they may feel pain. If we are happy with the way things are, if we feel comfortable and our existing strategies work, there is little motivation to change. It is *discomfort* with the existing situation, *pain* when all our usual strategies fail, that opens us to the possibility of change. To be really on top of things, a company has to be sensitive to some discomfort even when things are going well.

Deep, transformational change requires that we literally rewire our brains, that we grow new neural connections. That means we must *feel* the old wires being wrenched loose. We must feel in the pits of our stomachs all our old mental associations and their accompanying emotions being brought first to the surface of awareness and then restructured. Such processes raise our anxiety levels and require great courage if they are to be gone through to the end. All the great inspirational stories of transformation told throughout human history tell of nations or individuals going through what the Christian mystics called "a dark night of the soul"—Persephone's journey to the Underworld or Theseus's battle with the Minotaur in Greek mythology, Israel's forty years in the desert or Christ's forty days, the Buddha's weeks under the Bohdi tree. The central transformation story of Western culture is Christ's (and hence humanity's) rebirth only after death on the cross. *Ye must die that ye shall be reborn. You must lose your life that you may gain your life.*

At Motorola, the global communications company based in Chicago, the leaders are initiating an ambitious transformation program intended to embrace every employee in the company. Core company values, valued traditions of leadership, and the fundamental human skills required to make the company prosper are all being reinvented. New learning skills are being instilled through huge investment in learning research. Company education programs and learning skills are being exported into the community and the local school system in an effort to retrain tomorrow's employees, customers, and suppliers. "How long will all this take?" I asked. "A generation," was the answer. At Toshiba, they have a two-hundred-year transformation plan!

3

Yet we expect both personal and organizational transformation to be easy. Most companies demand hard evidence of a turnaround in one to five years. A quick read through a how-to book, a short management course on the challenges of change, or a brief spell of counseling or psychotherapy—better still, a pill or some "restructuring." Freud mentioned nearly a hundred years ago that all transformation processes are very slow and difficult, yet that his patients hoped to invest little time or energy. We are even less patient today, with our fixation on instant results.

As I was writing this book, I was reading another, Daniel Quinn's *Ishmael. Ishmael* is the story of a gorilla who becomes teacher to a human being who thinks he wants to save the world. At the very beginning of their lessons, Ishmael, the gorilla, tells his student that the teaching will be dangerous and difficult for him. The student, he says, has been told a story, the story of the origins and purpose of human life. Ishmael's teaching will call this story into question, with grave consequences for his student:

> This is the story that man was born to enact [Ishmael says], and to depart from it is to resign from the human race itself, is to venture into oblivion. . . . To step outside this story is to fall off the edge of the world . . . I want you to have at least a vague idea what you're getting into here. Once you learn to (hear this story being told all around you), humming in the background . . . you'll never stop being conscious of it. Wherever you go for the rest of your life, you'll be tempted to say to the people around you, 'How can you listen to this stuff and not recognize it for what it is?' And if you do this, people will look at you oddly and wonder what the devil you're talking about. In other words, if you take this educational journey with me, you're going to find yourself alienated from the people around you—friends, family, past associates, and so on.

Real corporate transformation will take companies and their leaders on a journey like that of Ishmael's pupil. Some may feel they are near to "falling off the edge of the world," but those who keep their nerve will enter another reality. They will see the corporate world and its opportunities with fresh eyes, and some will lay the foundations of tomorrow's corporate success stories.

The cultural story that most corporate leaders have bought into unawares has its origins in the scientific revolution of the sixteenth and seventeenth centuries. This revolution, the Newtonian revolution, brought with it a whole worldview and set of values that affected nearly every aspect of life. Philosophers, economists, psychologists, educators, and social theorists adopted this story. Through the influence of the engineer Frederick Taylor and his "Scientific Management" theory, this story came to dominate twentieth-century corporate thinking.

We live largely in a world of Newtonian organizations. These are organizations that thrive on certainty and predictability. They are hierarchical; power emanates from the top, and control is vital at every level. So, often, is fear. They are heavily bureaucratic and rule-bound, and hence inflexible. They stress the single point of view, the one best way forward. They are managed as though the part organizes the whole. Newtonian organizations do not respond well to change. Their primary value is efficiency. Human beings work and live in such organizations, but we often feel like passive units of production. Our lives serve the organizations, but the organizations serve only our utilitarian needs, and that only so long as we conform to the organization's purposes and are vital to the organization itself. The emphasis on control isolates these organizations from their environments. They don't interact with or respect those environments, including the people who work within them.

It is my purpose here to describe a wholly different kind of organization. I hope to offer a new model for structure, leadership, and learning within organizations that can thrive on uncertainty, can deal creatively with rapid change, and can release the full potential of the human beings who lead and work or live within them. Such organizations, like the human brain, have the potential for self-organizing creativity just waiting to be unleashed within them. This new model is based on the thinking, ideas, language, and imagery of the new science—quantum physics, chaos and complexity, and the latest brain science. I believe that understanding the philosophical basis of these sciences, understanding the new *paradigm* from which they emerge, is critical to rewiring the corporate brain.

In the pages that follow, we will try to understand the fundamental dynamics of transformation processes and why most transformation processes currently used in business fail. We will learn to recognize and describe the uses and limitations of traditional paradigms (the "paradigm paradox") in business activities and other life contexts. We will look at the three kinds of thinking that the human brain can do, how the first two of these are linked to familiar business processes and infrastructures, and how the third can enable us to rewire our brains and redesign our corporations. Eight fundamental principles of the new science will be discussed, and their application to business and leadership contrasted with the Newtonian approach. Understanding this contrast is critical to new corporate thinking.

Later in the book, we will look at Western and Eastern models of the self, or the person, and see how these have led to two different (and familiar) models of organization. In an attempt to synthesize and reach beyond the differences of West and East, we will look at a quantum model of self and organization drawn from the thinking of the new science. The process of dialogue will be discussed in depth as a practical tool for embedding the thinking of the new science and using it to rewire the corporate brain. And finally, a new model of the servant leader will be presented, a model that embraces the vision of the new science and illustrates the link between servant leadership, quantum thinking, and deep corporate transformation.

Much of the book contrasts the Newtonian and new science, or quantum, approaches to leadership. But this is not to convey a message of either-or. All the fundamental thinking of the new science is about both-and. The new science *incorporates* the old. Quantum physics does not invalidate Newtonian physics. It just shows that Newton's laws are restricted to one band of reality. But they are still necessary and useful. Newtonian thinking is as necessary to corporate leadership as the new paradigm, quantum thinking. The core competence I hope to convey in this book is about "managing at the edge"—that is, becoming aware that there are different paradigms and cultivating the judgment to know when to use one or another, or when to remain at the edge between the two.

I

Using the New Science to Rewire Corporate Thinking

S cience never exists in a vacuum; scientific thought and discovery grow out of the wider culture. Science focuses important trends in the wider culture through its precise language, imagery, and capacity for experiment. In turn, science then reaches forward to influence new developments in the wider culture. As we approach the new millennium, we live in a culture almost wholly underwritten by scientific thinking, scientific discovery, and the application of science through technology. This is not new, but the science of today is new and thus offers us a radically new cultural understanding. This applies to our corporations as much as to our societal and personal lives.

Since the seventeenth century, our dominant Western paradigm has been shaped by Newtonian science. This is true in management as well as in politics, economics, psychology, and education. Newtonian, or mechanistic, science is determinist, reductionist, and atomistic. Things happen because they *have* to happen; iron laws assure certainty and predictability. Any whole is best understood by reducing it to its constituent parts and looking at those parts in isolation. Reality consists of discrete, impenetrable particles relating to each other through forces of action and reaction. Newtonian truth is a simplistic either-or truth. There is one, best, god's-eye view of the universe. Nature is structured hierarchically, and there is an absolute split between the scientific observer and the world observed. Hence the stress on scientific objectivity, and the cult of the expert. The Newtonian organization has evolved within this paradigm.

Newtonian science is a product of the Western tradition. It developed many of the core ideas of early Greek philosophy and also those of Judeo-Christian monotheism. More particularly, Newtonian science reflects the cultural shift that shook the European tradition at the time of the Protestant Reformation, the growing Age of Rationalism (the Enlightenment), and the Cartesian revolution in thinking about mind, body, and reason. Like the Protestants who said to the Church, "Get out of my way. I'll relate to God directly, by myself," the mechanistic scientists said to the priests and the philosophers, "Don't *tell* us about nature. We'll find out." Where the rationalists looked for the laws of reason, the mechanists searched for the laws of nature. And where Descartes identified himself with the mind, the mechanists devoted themselves to studying the body, that is, physical nature.

Toward the end of the nineteenth century, this whole Western tradition began to unravel. Philosophers, artists, writers, even scientists lost their faith in reason's simplicity. As the British philosopher Isaiah Berlin expressed it, "There is not one truth that 'Reason' can agree." The German philosopher Nietzsche announced that "God is dead." He meant the old paradigm is dead. The framework that structured Western thinking no longer held. Cubist art challenged the single perspective (those Picasso paintings with the many faces pointing simultaneously in many different directions); modern art in general set out to break structure. The two Great Wars undermined our Enlightenment faith in human reason and human nature, existentialist philosophers questioned the possibility of objectivity, and the whole postmodernist movement set out to "deconstruct" the past. A new paradigm was being born.

The radically new science of the twentieth century—relativity, quantum mechanics, chaos, and complexity theory—helps us to see the basic outlines of this new paradigm. Like Newtonian science before it, twentieth-century science has grown out of a deep shift in general culture—a move away from absolute truth and absolute perspective, toward contextualism; a move away from certainty, toward an appreciation for pluralism and diversity, toward an acceptance of ambiguity and paradox, of complexity rather than simplicity. Also like Newtonian science, this new science sharply focuses the associated cultural shift and helps us to articulate the new paradigm. It provides us with the new concepts, new categories, new language, and new images that new paradigm thinking requires. Quantum thinking is new paradigm thinking. Both can help us rethink the structure and leadership of organizations, and underpin change processes that will allow business to thrive in the new paradigm.

1

Three Levels of Real Transformation

We know a great deal from science and psychology today about transformations in both physical and living systems. Many of these are universal, some are specific to living systems, and a few are specific to human beings because of our intelligence, complexity, and particular psychology. The human self has three levels: the mental, the emotional, and the spiritual—that deep layer of the self from which we are in touch with questions of meaning and value. It is crucial to emphasize here, and to remember through the remainder of this book, that *spiritual* need not have any religious associations. Human beings can be members of any religion or of no religion, and still have a spiritual layer.

In human beings, the mental aspect is those things we normally associate with explicit thinking, our ability to solve problems, to follow rules, to obtain goals. But *which* problems we choose to solve, what goals we think it *worth* obtaining, and our *willingness* to follow rules all spring from our emotional and spiritual aspects—from our aspirations, our ambitions, our associations, and our pain; from our visions and deepest values. Aspirations, ambitions, associations, and pain have obvious societal and emotional origins—social values, peer group pressure, personal relationships, childhood experience, and so on. But the latest depth psychology provides evidence that all are underpinned by our quest for meaning, by our visions and deepest values, that is, by our spiritual side.

10

Because organizations organize human beings, they, too, have mental, emotional, and spiritual aspects. The mental side of an organization is its overt thinking processes, its explicit rules, the reasoning used to set priorities and to achieve goals. In Newtonian organizations, with their emphasis on results and efficiency, this mental faculty has been split off. Such organizations ask, "What is the best (the cheapest, the most effective) way to do x?" They seldom ask, "Is x worth doing?" or "What does it *mean* that we are doing x? What does doing x mean for our employees or our customers or the wider community? Would it be better if we did y?" These are not purely mental questions. In organizations, as in human beings, the questions of what priorities to set or which goals to pursue are emotional and spiritual questions. They spring from the organization's basic vision.

In any human being or in any human organization, real change requires a fundamental shift at each of the three levels of the self. Change at any one level on its own is ineffective, yet most change processes do focus on just one level. Some appeal to our minds, some to our emotions, and a few to our spiritual level. The result is that people or organizations get out of balance, precocious in some ways, backward in others. For the whole system to thrive and change, progress must be balanced. Transformation must be experienced at all levels.

The human self does not consist of a series of little boxes separately labeled "Mind," "Heart," and "Spirit." No more does an organization consist of a series of smaller divisions separately labeled "Product Development," "Marketing," "Finance," and so on. Both are Newtonian models based on the premise that the world consists of atomistic, separate little bits. Freud took these models into psychology, Frederick Taylor introduced them to management. In both cases they have led to notions that change or transformation can happen piecemeal, working on different parts of the system independently.

Today, we should know better. All the sciences of the twentieth century, both physical and biological, are holistic. They show that the world does not consist of separate, isolated parts but rather of intricately interrelated systems. A change in any one apparent part affects the whole. Quantum physics tells us that the universe actually consists of patterns of dynamic energy, self-organizing wave patterns like so many whirlpools, the boundaries of each interlaced with those of all the others. If we could look through a quantum microscope, the whole effect would look like the interlocking patterns of waves on the sea. From chaos theory we learn about the famous "butterfly effect"—the world's physical systems are so interrelated that sometimes the mere flapping of a butterfly's wings in Beijing is enough to cause a tornado to form over Kansas City. At our own level of daily reality, such holism has been brought home to us most forcefully in our understanding of the complex and interrelated factors that have contributed to our current environmental crisis. Both the latest research in human psychology and the systems approach in management thinking have taken such insights on board. Some of the newer economists realize it. There are no high walls around the world's apparently separate systems. There are no hard boundaries around separate parts of the self. Our mental, emotional, and spiritual aspects are interwoven, each feeding—and feeding on—the others. The same is true of the supposedly separate divisions of our organizations.

Western culture has always had this propensity to split things up into little boxes. It goes back to the atomism of the ancient Greeks. But there has been an accompanying and equally distorting Western tendency to split the mind or soul off from the body, or the spiritual from the physical. Both the early Greeks and the Christian Church taught such dualism. In the seventeenth century, the French philosopher René Descartes gave this a very modern twist by saying, "I know that I have a mind, and I know that I have a body. And I know that the two are completely separate. I *am* my mind. I *have* a body." Isaac Newton took this split as the basis of his new physics, excluding everything mental or psychological from his new physical laws of the universe. The mechanistic culture to which his physics gave rise, the culture that still dominates the thinking of most of us today, applies the Newtonian categories of the machine to human beings and to human organizations.

Freud looked for the "laws and dynamics" that governed the psyche and insisted that human behavior was fully determined by such laws and their interaction with early experience. Adam Smith looked for the laws and principles that guide the market economy and insisted we could use them to predict and control market behavior. In management theory, the engineer Frederick Taylor insisted that every organization is bound by underlying laws and principles and that the human beings within the organization act accordingly. Discover your company's underlying laws and you can work with them to predict and control the behavior of your markets, your employees, and your production. In the more modern language of our computer culture, the whole thing is *programmed*.

Iron laws, prediction, control, programs. These are the bywords of Newtonian physics and mechanistic culture. They are key words in Newtonian management thinking. But how accurately do they describe today's world or meet the needs of today's companies? How do we predict and control complexity? How do we program chaos? Where are the iron laws that guarantee the behavior (and therefore the creativity and the productivity) of what managers are beginning to call "intellectual capital"? How do we quantify and measure the more human characteristics and uniquely human potential in those people that managers now rightly describe as their companies' "greatest assets" or their "competitive advantage"?

Human beings do have mechanical aspects. Our muscles work very much like machines and indeed it was human muscles that the technology of the Industrial Revolution began to replace. There are also mechanical aspects of our minds, aspects that are indeed programmed. Our rational, rule-bound, problem-solving, goal-oriented thinking operates very like the program of an ordinary personal computer (PC). And it is these mechanical aspects of our minds that computers are replacing in large numbers. The corporate world does not need more human "thinking machines." Silicon chips are cheaper, faster, and more reliable. The "intellectual capital" that companies want to develop today involves those aspects of human beings that *no* machine can duplicate, those special qualities of people that can't be programmed.

Computers don't have emotions. They don't feel pain, they don't laugh at jokes, they don't write poems, they certainly don't have spiritual needs and insight. Human beings do all these things because we have emotional and spiritual sides. These are the things that link the human self with its world. Computers don't *have* selves. In human beings, thinking is not split off from emotion and spirit—our creativity and uniqueness depends upon these more complex sides of the self. So does our capacity to have vision, to dream, and to assign meaning to our projects.

13

Reflecting on the kinds of existential choices he has had to make during the course of his personal life and leadership career, Marks & Spencer's Andrew Stone makes another crucial distinction between ourselves and computers. "It seems to me," he says, "that at one time or another we humans have to face the choice of dying or of carrying on. If we can't face death, we have to *justify* to ourselves a reason for being alive, for surviving. If this is a truly deep justification, it has meaning, and it becomes our *raison d'être,* our reason for carrying on." For Stone, as we shall see later, this deep reason for staying alive became the driving vision behind his leadership in retailing. Computers don't make such life-and-death choices.

Equally, just as vision is inseparable from our spiritual intelligence, our capacity to handle ambiguity, uncertainty, and complexity is bound up with our "emotional intelligence." So is our capacity to work on teams. Our striving, our drive toward perfection, our dedication, and our need to serve are bound up with our "spiritual intelligence." And these are the human qualities for which organizations must make room—indeed must nurture—if they want to unleash the full potential of human creativity and productivity.

An organization must nurture three kinds of intelligence:
- Mental intelligence
- Emotional intelligence
- Spiritual intelligence

Ironically, it is these very qualities of emotional and spiritual intelligence that many corporate transformation programs strive to develop. At least they try to tap into the *net result* of their employees having such qualities. Most corporate leaders today would like to have a workforce, or at least a managerial team, that can think on its feet, be creative, thrive on complexity, take responsibility, and give its all to the firm. This is why they are spending millions on so-called change agents, consultants who specialize in managing transformation. But most change agents are themselves mechanistic and haven't a clue what deep transformation means, never mind what it requires. Most don't know where to begin, so they satisfy themselves with downsizing or "restructuring," with introducing a "change vocabulary," with charts that say "vision" and "value" and "leadership." They give two-day or two-week seminars on "creativity." But they don't "change the room"—they work within the *existing* structures. And Newtonian organizations have no existing structures that allow emotional intelligence to develop, never mind structures that foster spiritual vision. Newtonian organizations have no inner capacity for fundamental transformation.

The Need for a New Leadership Psychology

Most people who think about the challenges facing management and leadership know that something is stuck. The consultants and the gurus introduce one gimmick after another, and unwittingly maintain mechanistic assumptions about human behavior derived from the old physical sciences and their methodology. Thus the unceasing attempts to analyze and measure motivation and personality in order to use them as predictive tools, and the common belief that there are measurable criteria (and hence an applicable technique) for becoming a more effective leader, a better person, a good counselor, a creative individual. What CEO would pay for anything less? Thus the two-day or two-week seminars on transformation that transform nothing.

Some training managers and consultants concerned with individual or leadership development are familiar with and use American psychologist Abraham Maslow's famous "Hierarchy of Needs" (shown in Figure 1) to chart their way through the human psyche. It is one of the best and most wide-ranging models of human priorities and hence human motivation ever to be summed up in one table, and it commonly appears in the textbooks or handout booklets of change-management courses. Formed in the shape of a pyramid, human needs are divided into the "basic needs" of survival, safety, and security, and then the "growth needs" of belonging (social), esteem (ego), and self-actualization. By self-actualization, Maslow meant the need for meaning, the deep need to feel that one's life and work are *about* something, the spiritual aspect of the self. Over the years the psychological insight of the corporate world has slowly been working its way up Maslow's pyramid.

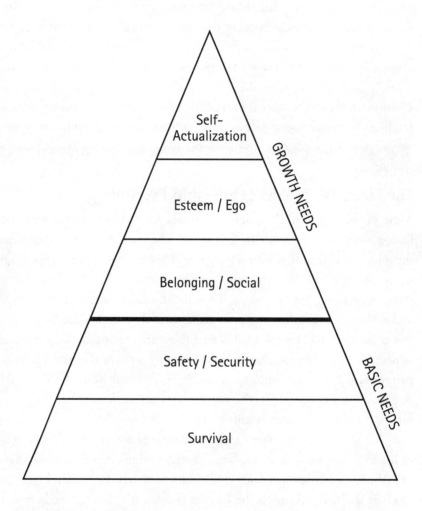

Figure 1.   Maslow's Hierarchy of Needs

The labor unions (themselves heavily Newtonian organizations) were the first to fight for recognition of employees' basic needs for survival and security—safety measures, adequate pay, rest breaks, and so on. These are needs common in some form or another to any living organism, human or otherwise, and thus take no special account of the human dimension in organizations. The union reforms were necessary but not sufficient. It was for the later Human Relations Movement and its assorted transformation schemes to stress the importance of the higher, or "growth needs"; the need for work to have a personal dimension, the need for individuals to have a sense of self-esteem, the need to foster better relationships at work, the need for work-site counseling, and so on. Some of this made some difference to people's tolerance or even enjoyment of work, but again it was not sufficient to deliver deep transformation. People at work could smile at each other sometimes, they could leave their babies in crèches provided by the boss, they could vent their frustration to a counselor. But organizations have remained stressful places, loneliness prevails, fear still drives the relationship between subordinates and their bosses, risk is still not adequately rewarded. From the point of view of an organization's long-term success, nothing important has changed. Thinking remains stuck, experimentation remains tentative, inflexible organizational structures still thwart human potential, and the organization as a whole resists change.

It is only very recently that Maslow's last category, the need for self-actualization, has touched business circles—among the few who begin to see the need for a more spiritual dimension in business, who see that initiative and creativity within companies, and even the ultimate survival *of* companies, is bound up with core meaning and values. These are the people who need a new, more complex psychological model that links the mental, emotional, and spiritual intelligence of employees, at the very least of managers. And they need a vision of how to use their new understanding to change the priorities, the structure, and the leadership of organizations.

The Maslow hierarchy is good. It does at least recognize that human beings have a range of needs and that the need for meaning is one of them. But the model is upside down and too hierarchical. It does not answer the need for a new corporate psychology. Maslow makes the basic need for safety and security (that is, a category of material things) the foundation of his pyramid, stressing that it is the sine qua non for sustaining life. He places self-actualization (meaning) at the apex, the ultimate goal of the fulfilled life—nice if you can get it, but really just the icing on the cake. Other needs are ranked in between. This ranking of priorities mirrors the bottom-line-returns bias of Western corporate culture (immediate stockholder value), and that in turn mirrors the generally materialist bias of Western culture itself. It also atomizes needs into hierarchical boxes, giving the false impression that we can rank and separate physical, personal, social, and spiritual needs. Human beings are more holistic than that. So, too, would be organizations that can use full human potential to thrive on change and complexity.

In this book I am going to argue that we need to invert Maslow's pyramid. *The need for meaning is primary.* There are countless documented instances of people sacrificing comfort, companionship, food, even life itself in pursuit of meaning, higher morality, or higher ideals. In the corporate world, there are countless examples of employees agreeing to longer hours and less pay if they can see that this is for the greater good of all, or in the pursuit of some goal that excites them. The people who survived prisoner of war and concentration camps in World War II were the people most motivated by deeply held beliefs and values. Productivity levels in automobile plants have been increased by putting people on small teams that build whole cars, so that each employee has a vision of the purpose of the work and the satisfaction of seeing it completed.

It is also true that the need for meaning cannot be separated from what might be called lesser needs for security, material well-being, companionship, and self-esteem. Each level of the self suffuses every other level. The self is a dynamic system and our needs support each other in a dynamic way. The same is true in organizations. We cannot split off an organization's need for profit from its need to give employees self-esteem nor from its need for deep vision. So many things go wrong in organizations because we don't understand this basic holistic, systemic aspect of their structure.

Throughout this book I am going to replace Maslow's pyramidal Hierarchy of Needs with the set of interlocking concentric circles shown in Figure 2. I shall place spiritual needs (vision, value, meaning) at the center, stressing that this class underpins and suffuses everything else, but I also want to portray the dynamic interplay between our different needs, the different aspects of our selves, the different goals, pursuits, and internal structures of our organizations. I am also going to stress throughout the book that all fundamental transformation is ultimately *spiritual* transformation, spiritual in the very broadest sense as issuing from the level of reflection, meaning, and value. This is true for individuals and for companies. It is also crucially true that creative thinking emerges from this spiritual level, whether it is thinking about widgets, thinking about orga-nizational structures, or thinking about long-term strategies and purposes.

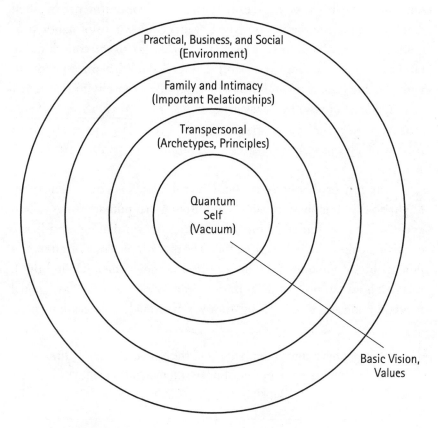

Figure 2.   Layers of the Self
Source: © 1996, Ian Marshal.

In corporate language, the spiritual level is the company's basic vision. Vision does not mean "our plans for the next five years" or "how we plan to achieve our goals." It is more basic than that. A company's vision is its overall—and often *unconscious*—sense of identity, its aspira-tions, its sense of itself in the wider world, its deeper, motivating core val-ues and long-term strategies. In one example I often use with senior managers at Shell, I ask them whether they see Shell as an oil company or as an energy company. The answer to that is a key to the company's core vision. The two answers are very different and each would lead to a different set of long-term aims and prospects, different research and development strategies, a different sense of Shell's role in the larger economy and in the global community, a different sense of identity and purpose (and hence a different degree of loyalty and commitment) in Shell employees. If Shell or other companies want genuine transformation programs, they must start at that level. They must get to the core thinking (and being!) that can reach and shift that level. And they must maintain, with suitable leadership and infrastructures, their capacity to tap freshly into that level of vision whenever necessary. *A company, like an individual, must always be able to access its spiritual core.* That is the only level from which it can shift its existing assumptions, leadership patterns, and structures.

The rest of this book is about how leaders and their companies might do this. It is about the kinds of thinking that human beings can do and the level of thinking from which deep transformation, and hence creativity, issues. We will explore together the complex organization and potentiality of the human brain (and its accompanying self), and think together how nature's best organization yet devised can be used as a model for rethinking and restructuring our own man-made organizations.

> The organization, potentiality, and thinking processes of the human brain are our most powerful model for creative thinking in organizations.

Creativity and Quantum Thinking

Creative thinking, the thinking that originates crucially from the spiritual level of the self, issues from a brain dynamic that functions very like the processes and systems described by quantum physics and the other new sciences. Some brain scientists even believe that there is an actual quantum level in the brain, perhaps coupled with "chaotic" activity, that makes creative thinking possible. Whether that is true remains to be proved. But human creativity is so similar to the creativity of quantum processes that I find it useful to call creative thinking *quantum thinking.* For similar reasons, I often refer to the spiritual level of the self as *the quantum self.* This allows us to find a language, a set of images, and even an organizational model for nurturing creativity and creative leadership in the existing language, imagery, and organization of quantum and chaotic systems and the quantum brain.

The essence of quantum physics is that it describes an unfixed, both-and level of reality that thrives on ambiguity and uncertainty at something very like "the edge of chaos." The essence of the quantum self is that it describes that origin of the self that precedes divisions into mind and body, into the mental and the emotional, and that precedes the self's identification with existing ways to be. The quantum self is not an off-the-peg self, not a persona or a mask. The essence of quantum thinking is that it is the thinking that precedes categories, structures, and accepted patterns of thought, or mind-sets. It is with quantum thinking that we create our categories, change our structures, and transform our patterns of thought. Quantum thinking is vital to creative thinking and leadership in organizations. It is the key to any genuine organizational transformation. It is the key to shifting our paradigm. Quantum thinking is the link between the brain's creativity, organizational transformation and leadership, and the ideas found in the new science.

Product development in business lies somewhere on a grid of criss-crossing influences that link pure science and fine art with technology (applied science) and design (applied art). Quantum thinking drives pure science and fine art; paradigm shifts in technology give rise to new products.

The Need to Shift Paradigms

Many businesspeople are familiar with the word *paradigm,* but I believe that few really understand it. Paradigm is another of those greatly overused, misused, and abused words that have become part of the gobbledygook of the "change vocabulary." Some people think it means a mental model or a mind-set, some use it as though it is just a new idea or a set of ideas, a set of habits, a style, or even a set of traditions or prejudices. A paradigm does include all these things, but it is much more.

Our paradigm, used in the proper sense first defined by American philosopher of science Thomas Kuhn in *The Structure of Scientific Revolutions,* is the whole conceptual framework embracing our most deeply held, unconscious assumptions and values. It is the things we take for granted in any situation. Like a pair of glasses that we wear to focus our visual world, our paradigm focuses the whole of our mental and emotional reality. It determines our expectations, frames the questions that we will ask, and structures our approach to what we do. Paradigms are so deep that they even determine what we will see. When people who lived in the Middle Ages went to the seashore, for instance, they literally did not see the curvature of the horizon. To us it's obvious because we know (we have the paradigm) that the earth is round, but they knew the earth was flat. So a curved horizon would have made no sense to them, they had no categories to see it, and thus they *didn't* see it. Nor, it follows, did they ask questions like, "Why don't we fall off?" That kind of question is raised by our paradigm of the round earth.

Our Paradigm

- Our most deeply held, unconscious set of assumptions and values
- The things we take for granted
- That which determines our expectations, frames the questions we ask, and structures our approach to what we do

---

We can't help having paradigms. Indeed, we need them. They are literally wired into our brains so that we have the concepts and categories necessary to digest our experience. Philosophers and neuroscientists used to think that we are *hard wired*—born with certain neural connections that frame our experience from birth and remain with us throughout our lives. This view was accompanied by the notion that we have a limited learning horizon related to aging and that beyond a certain age (about eighteen) our capacities diminish. But we know today this is not true.

Today neuroscience teaches that from the moment of conception until the end of life itself we have the constant capacity to grow new neural connections. When we come into the world as infants, we come with very little of our brain wired up. We are born with sufficient neural connections to regulate our breathing, our body temperature, and the beating of our heart, but nearly everything else is pure potentiality. What diet we will be fed, what climatic conditions and germs we will encounter, what language we will need to speak, what social and practical skills we will need to learn, what concepts we will need to form—all these are uncertain at the moment of birth. So the infant's brain is poised at the edge. Chaotic instability in its initial neural firings enables the brain to adapt to whatever physical and cultural conditions it finds. It allows the brain to wire itself as it evolves with experience.

Experiments have been done, for instance, on the language-learning abilities of human infants. The sounds that infants make in the first months of birth have been recorded, and psychologists have discovered that every human infant, everywhere on this planet, utters all eight hundred or so phonemes (sound patterns) found in the totality of *all* human languages. The infant's brain ranges across the whole spectrum of all possible languages. Yet within the first year of life, infants select out those phonemes relevant to the language of their own culture. They lay down neural pathways for recognizing and using those sounds—they wire their brains according to their environment—and lose the ability to recognize and use the sounds not used by the surrounding culture.

Infants and children lay down new neural connections—wire their brains—of necessity and at a rapid rate. They have to construct their world. Older people may be able to get by on the experience of their first eighteen years, may be able to sleepwalk through life. It is tempting to do so because growing new neural connections requires energy and can be painful. When we think creatively, the brain uses more energy than the whole rest of the body. But we are not condemned to be sleepwalkers. Given a motivation, given an opportunity, given a crisis, we can and do grow new neural connections at any age. Experiments have shown that people well into their nineties still have the capacity to rewire their brains.

Thomas Kuhn wrote about paradigms to describe how scientists work. We usually think of science as very revolutionary, "at the edge." But Kuhn pointed out that most normal science is very conservative. Most scientists work from within a paradigm and most of their experiments are done to validate that paradigm. New ideas are not welcome and are treated at first as anomalies. It is only when the anomalies, the things that won't fit the old paradigm, mount up that "revolutionary science" takes over. Revolutionary science *changes* the paradigm. It has the insight and the courage to say that the old way of looking at things won't work. But such revolutions are painful. The necessary casualty is our whole way of looking at things.

We need a paradigm to function at all, but the danger is that we can get trapped inside our paradigm. Then new thinking becomes impossible. This is the "paradigm paradox." Science cannot be changed from within its old paradigm; neither can business. To change the rules of the game we have to step outside the rules. In the same way, we can't transform the structures of organizations from within the existing structures. This is difficult for those who have grown up within the existing structures and have invested their whole careers in learning how to use them. Kuhn argued that a scientific paradigm couldn't shift until all the practitioners of the old paradigm died. This may be too bleak, but to change our paradigm we do have to rewire our brains and, like scientists, we are usually motivated to do so only when catastrophe strikes, when the old structures simply won't work anymore. I think this is where we have got to today, in politics, economics, education, and business. *Our old structures just don't work.*

The Paradigm Paradox

We need our paradigms to make sense of the world, yet because of these we become trapped or constrained.

Business leaders, too, like scientists, have their paradigm—their deeply held and largely unconscious set of assumptions and values, the questions they think it natural to ask, the experiments they think it reasonable to do. This paradigm is shared with the wider culture and has grown out of our whole Western tradition. It has been focused sharply by the language, concepts, and categories of mechanistic science and includes basic assumptions like force, causality, predictability, and what should be taken for granted. Thus business leaders couch their analyses and future scenarios in language referring to market forces, market forecasts, chains of cause and effect ("If we do this, x will react like that"), and "best possible" practices and solutions. Power and control are central features of this paradigm. Efficiency is one of its central values.

If we want to transform the structure and leadership of our organizations, we have to address change at this fundamental paradigmatic level. We have to change the thinking behind our thinking. Leaders who want to initiate real change processes must become aware that they have been acting out of a paradigm. They must see the origin and nature of this existing paradigm and its effect on their management. And they must get to a point where they can *feel* the reality of an alternative paradigm—or the creative excitement of standing at the edge between paradigms. They must learn to ask fundamentally new questions, to bring themselves to a point where their very categories of thought and vision are different. They must come to see themselves, the world, human relations, and their companies in a fundamentally new way. If they can reach this point, then they will be in a position to change the room rather than shifting the same old furniture about in it. Changing the room means seeing and implementing the possibility of a fundamentally new form of organization. It means learning to think in a new way—to use *all* of the brain's capacity for thought. As we shall see next, this means learning to think and to implement three kinds of thinking.

2

Three Kinds of Thinking:

How the Brain Rewires Itself

The brain is the most complex organ in the body. The brain somehow produces the mystery of conscious mind, our awareness of ourselves and our world. It generates and structures our thoughts, enables us to have emotions, and somehow mediates our spiritual lives—our sense of meaning and value. The brain gives us touch, sight, smell, and language. It controls the beating of our hearts, the rate at which we sweat, the pace of our breathing, and countless other bodily functions. Its outward-reaching neural fibers extend to every region of the body. It is the bridge between our inner lives and the outer world. The brain can do all these things because it is flexible, adaptive, and self-organizing. It constantly rewires itself.

The human brain is capable of three distinctive kinds of thinking. Ian Marshall published the foundation work on this concept in 1996, as a chapter in *Towards a Scientific Basis for Consciousness,* edited by S. Hameroff and others.

Rational, logical, rule-bound thinking produces concepts and categories similar to those found in the Newtonian particle paradigm. Associative, habit-bound thinking gives us pattern-recognizing abilities that are very similar to the Newtonian wave paradigm—everything is interlinked. Creative, rule-breaking, and rule-making thinking behaves very like the emergent structures found in the quantum paradigm. These three kinds of thinking and their associated brain structures provide a powerful model that companies can emulate when looking for infrastructures that can thrive on change and harness meaning.

The brain is nature's most complex and multifaceted organization. All man-made organizations are in fact reflections of this natural template. Man-made organizations are approximations of the real thing based on their leaders' best ability to draw on the full resources of nature's potential. If leaders deepen their understanding of this potential—if they raise their own consciousness of brain dynamics, structure, and capacity—they will be better placed to rewire the corporate brains of the companies they lead.

The Brain's Infinite Capacity to Grow

As I said earlier, scientists used to think that the brain is hard wired. We are born with a certain number of neurons connected in particular ways, so the theory went, and with aging the whole network slowly deteriorates. People were thought to be in their mental prime at about age eighteen, after which it was downhill all the way! Today neuroscientists know better. True, we are born with a certain number of neurons and we do constantly lose these as we go through life. An older person has far fewer neurons than a baby. But we constantly grow neural connections, or at least we have the capacity to do so.

It is neural connections that give us our mental capacities. The more complex and varied those capacities, the more neural connections we need. The human infant is born with the basic necessities for maintaining life—neural connections to regulate breathing, heartbeat, temperature, and so on. But infants do not yet have the capacity to see faces and objects, to form concepts, to utter coherent sounds. These capacities evolve over time as experience enriches the infant brain's capacity. Through experience of the world, the brain lays down new neural connections. The richer and more varied that experience, the greater the maze of neural connections that forms. This is why we know now that we can boost infant intelligence and even physical coordination through offering frequent and varied stimulation—brightly colored objects to look at, different sounds and voices, a range of things to smell and taste, back rubs, and emotional warmth.

Infants *must* grow new neural connections in their brains if they are to have a world. Early connections provide the capacity to recognize tastes, smells, faces, and voices. With increasing maturity, new neural connections allow language and concept formation; they store the facts and experiences of memory, they enable reading, writing, and general learning. There is *no limit* to how many neural connections a child's brain can grow. But in our culture, by about the age of sixteen or eighteen (early twenties if the child continues with higher education), most of us have grown enough neural connections to coast for the rest of our lives. We've formed an overall picture of our world and its ways. We have formed (and wired in) assumptions on which we can act. We've formed mental habits and emotional patterns, patterns of response to people and situations. In short, we've wired in our basic life's paradigm.

Growing new neural connections for the brain's initial wiring takes a lot of energy, but the child is motivated by both need and curiosity. And children do have a lot of energy. As adults we are less motivated. After all, we have all those habits and assumptions to call upon when dealing with experience. As long as our initial paradigm makes sense and copes with our basic needs, why change it? We have an infinite, lifelong capacity to lay down new neural connections, to change and grow our brains, but few of us use it. *Re*wiring the brain, challenging all those initial habits and assumptions in the face of new experience, requires far more energy than the original wiring. Rewiring means making the effort of deconstructing (tearing out!) all the old connections as well as laying down new ones. We resist it. So long as no great challenge rocks the boat, we resist spending energy we could save. But if things have gone badly wrong in our lives, if our original mental and emotional habits and our deeply held assumptions can no longer cope with some new challenge or experience, we *have* to rewire, or go under.

Thomas Kuhn pointed out that this is the way things happen in science, too. As I noted earlier, science has a reputation for being very revolutionary, always turning out cutting-edge breakthroughs. But Kuhn showed that this perception is wrong. Most science, he demonstrated, is intensely conservative—as anyone who has ever tried to publish a new idea in an established scientific journal can verify! "Normal scientists," as Kuhn refer to the vast body of conservative scientists, spend most of their careers trying to *ratify* their existing theories, their existing paradigm. Their experiments are designed to prove themselves right. If something turns up in an experiment that does not fit the mainstream theory, they assume a mistake has been made. They call the errant data an anomaly. In business or economics, such violations of mainstream theory or practice are called blips, accidents, or temporary distortions.

Conservative science (and conservative business practice) is of course valuable. Most new ideas, like most of the new mutations in biology, are no good. They get filtered out by the challenges of conservative people in the field. But these challenges can be *too* conservative. "Revolutionary science" takes off when someone has the vision and the courage to break the mold. A Copernicus, a Newton, an Einstein looks at those anomalies and sees a whole new way to look at the world. The Establishment listens—eventually!—only because its own way of looking at the world has broken down. In the corporate world, this is the point at which most companies seek transformation schemes, when internal crisis or challenge from the market has given them a make-or-break motivation to change. Addressing his general merchandise managers' conference on the theme of "Growing the Business," Andrew Stone of Marks & Spencer described growth in childhood or in crisis as the easy part of managing change.

"Growth's not difficult when you're small," he said. "Babies do it all the time. My children do it in their sleep! Actually getting up to a higher level when you've slipped down to the bottom is also not that difficult. Small growth companies and companies repairing themselves after a fall are referred to by the City [of London] as 'recovery stocks.' They love them!"

But growth and change are possible in good times, too. A company doesn't have to be on its knees before opening its brain to something new. As Stone pointed out, children do it all the time, as a matter of course. Creative adults are often noted for their childlike enthusiasm. And such adults very often look and feel younger than their peers. Britain's Richard Branson has maintained his boyish grin and sense of play well into middle age. Interestingly enough, one of the three criteria Branson applies when assessing whether to add some new venture to his Virgin Group is, Will it challenge authority?

A spirit of play, a spirit of rebelliousness, a sense of adventure, an eagerness to challenge and be challenged, these are the things that expose our brains to those experiences that make us grow new neural connections. But when a leader is already running a successful business, it takes a special kind of courage to remain childlike. As Andrew Stone went on to say, "When you are grown up and have reached a level you have never dreamt of, and you want to develop and climb still further, this is hard. This takes guts. It means knowing who you are and recognizing your strengths and building on them." And crucially, for people in business, it means keeping a constant eye on how the company can convert its sense of play, its vision, and its principles into products that sell. Both Marks & Spencer and Virgin are very good at that.

Mess, Wonderful Mess

Opening one of his leadership conferences, Phil Carroll, the CEO of Shell USA, advised his colleagues, "The world is a messy place. If we want to stay on top of the corporate ladder, we must plunge into the mess. We must learn to work with the mess."

The human brain is at the top of nature's intelligence ladder (so far as we know!), and it definitely got there by learning to work with mess. There is nothing planned or orderly about the brain's structure. This is just one of the things that makes it so difficult to study. Its architecture is a bit like the twisting alleyways and jumbled buildings of a medieval city, layer upon layer of archeological history built one on top of the other and all somehow being lived in. The brain's architecture—its neural wiring— carries within itself the whole history of the evolution of life on this planet, at least that belonging to the animal kingdom. And we use it all.

In the simplest layer of our nervous system, the part corresponding to the prehistory of the medieval city, we find structures like those of one-celled animals such as the amoeba or paramecium. They have no nervous system; all the sensory coordination and motor reflexes of these animals exist within one cell. Our own white blood cells, as they scavenge up rubbish and eat bacteria, behave in the bloodstream much like amoebas in ponds. Simple many-celled animals like jellyfish still have no central nervous system, but they do have a network of nerve fibers that allow communication between cells so that the animal can react in a coordinated way. In our bodies, the nerve cells in the gut form a network that coordinates peristalsis, the muscular contractions that push food along.

With the evolution of mammals a forebrain developed—first the primitive forebrain of the lower mammals, ruled primarily by instinct and emotion, and then the cerebral hemispheres with all their sophisticated computing ability, the "little gray cells" that most of us identify with the human mind. Yet drunkenness, the use of tranquilizers, or damage to the higher forebrain results in regression to primitive, more spontaneous, less calculating types of behavior of the kind found in lower mammals.

So despite the increasing centralization and complexity of the nervous system as it evolves, even in humans the more primitive nerve nets remain, both within our expanded brain and throughout the body. The more recent phases of our evolution have supplanted earlier phases but they have not entirely replaced them. The experience of the amoeba, the jellyfish, the earthworm, and the ant are all embedded in our nervous tissue. So, too, are the mental and emotional processes and responses of the rat, the wolf, the bear, and the cat embedded in our higher faculties. *We think with the whole history of evolution sleeping within each thought and in each act of the imagination.*

Our usual business-world model of "thinking," then, is inadequate to the real thing. Thinking is not an entirely cerebral process. It is not something we do best when we can be entirely cool and rational and detached. It is certainly not something we do simply and straightforwardly. We do think only with our heads—we also think with our emotions and our bodies and our spirits (our visions, our hopes, our sense of meaning and value). We think with all the complex and varied and messy nerve nets woven throughout our organisms. Everyday language recognizes this fact when we say things like, "He thinks with his guts," or "She thinks with her heart." Many leaders speak of having a "feel for the situation," described sometimes as almost "tactile."

Because the business world (like so much of the wider Western culture) has a limited picture of thinking, the structures evolved within organizations to encourage thinking, effective action, and success are also limited. Not surprisingly, the brain's thinking structures are more varied, taking into account the inputs from emotion, the body, and the spirit. Today, neuroscience knows that the three kinds of thinking involved in our higher mental faculties each employs a different kind of neural structure and processing in the brain. Let's look at these in depth to see what they might say to business thinking.

SERIAL THINKING: THE BRAIN'S "INTELLECT"

Our simplistic model of "thinking" as something straightforward, logical, and dispassionate is not wrong. It is just a part of the story. It is a model derived from formal logic and arithmetic—"If x, then y," or "2 + 2 = 4." Human beings are very good at this kind of thinking. PCs are even better at it. They can do it more accurately and more quickly than we can. The brain can do it because of one very distinctive sort of neural wiring known as *neural tracts.*

Neural tracts are neurons connected one-on-one in a series, like a series of telephone cables. The head of one neuron connects to the tail of the next one, and an electrochemical signal passes along the chain of linked neurons being employed for any particular thought or series of thoughts. Each neuron is switched either on or off, and if any neuron in the chain gets damaged or switched off, the whole chain ceases to function, like a chain of Christmas tree lights wired serially. PCs are wired in this serial fashion.

Neural tracts learn (are wired) according to a fixed program, the rules of which are laid down in accordance with formal logic. The learning involved is thus step-by-step and rule-bound. When we teach children their times tables by rote, we are encouraging them to wire their brains for serial processing. It produces a kind of thinking useful for solving problems or achieving tasks. It is goal-oriented, or instrumental, how-to thinking. It is the kind of thinking with which we manage the rules of grammar or the rules of a game. It is rational, logical thinking—"If I do this, then I know that a certain consequence will follow."

A great deal of the thinking involved in business is serial thinking. The analysis phase of an enterprise relies on breaking a situation down into its simplest logical parts and then predicting the causal relationships that will emerge. Strategic planning assumes a game plan and a step-by-step rationale for enacting it. "Management by objectives" assumes we set clear goals and objectives and then work out a logical series of actions for achieving them. Serial computers that play chess do so by analyzing all possible outcomes of each position and then calculating the strongest, step-by-step.

Like the kind of thinking that underpins Newtonian particle science, both the structures of and the thinking produced by neural tracts are linear and deterministic. B always follows A in the same way. This kind of thinking does not tolerate nuance or ambiguity. It is strictly on-off, either-or thinking. Fantastically effective within its set of given rules (within its program), the serial thinking process breaks down if someone moves the goal posts. It is like a PC asked to do a task not covered by its program. In that case, a message flashes on the screen to tell us "system not operating." In the metaphor of James Carse, serial thinking is "finite," it functions within boundaries. It is of no use when we need to scan the horizon for possibilities or when we have to deal with the unexpected.

Companies have many successful structures in place that embody serial thinking. The eight-hour shift itself, the time clock that signs employees in and out, the job descriptions and codes of dress, the whole bureaucratic structure describing responsibilities, codes of practice, holiday schedules, coffee breaks, and sickness benefits—all these are defined by rules applying generally to everyone within set categories. Serial thinking underlies the factory-floor blueprint or the engineer's repair manual. As I said, it underlies the analysis process in strategic planning or managing by objectives. All serial thinking accepts the assumption that the corporate world consists of parts (people, nuts and bolts, markets, customers, competitors) who can be manipulated successfully through rules and five-year plans because they are themselves predictable in their behavior, just as the Newtonian universe is governed by fixed Laws of Nature.

The advantages of serial thinking are that it is fast, accurate, precise, and reliable. The chief disadvantage is that it can only operate within a given paradigm, within a given program or set of rules. Similarly, the advantages of serial structures within organizations are that they are accurate, reliable, and universal. The disadvantage is that they are inflexible.

ASSOCIATIVE THINKING: THE BRAIN'S "HEART"

The second kind of thinking we can do is associative, or *parallel thinking*.

It helps us to form associations between things like hunger and the food that will satisfy it, between the need for comfort and the love we receive from others, between the color red and emotions of excitement or danger. Associative thinking also enables us to recognize patterns like faces or smells, and to learn bodily skills like riding a bicycle or driving a car.

The neural structures within the brain with which we do associative thinking are known as *neural networks*. Each of these networks contains bundles of up to a hundred thousand neurons, and each single neuron in the bundle may be connected to as many as a thousand others. The connections between neurons are random, messy, or parallel—that is, each neuron acts upon and is acted upon by many others simultaneously. The neural networks in the brain are connected to further neural networks located throughout the brain and the body. Associative thinking is thus rooted in our emotional and physical experience. It is "thinking" with the heart and the body.

Unlike serial neural tracts, neural networks have the ability to wire and rewire themselves in dialogue with experience. Each time I see a pattern, the neural network connections that recognize that pattern grow stronger, until recognition becomes something automatic. If the pattern alters, my ability to perceive it will slowly alter, too, until my brain has rewired itself to see the new pattern.

When I learn to drive a car, for instance, every move of my hands and feet is thoughtful and deliberate, and my control of the car is only slight. With each practice run, coordination between hands, feet, and brain is more strongly wired into the brain's neural networks (their interconnections grow stronger) until, eventually, I don't think about driving at all unless there is some unusual problem. Indeed, it even becomes *impossible* to think consciously, or at least easily, about my driving skills. Recently, my twelve-year-old son asked me, "Mum, what foot do you use to press the clutch pedal?" I couldn't answer him. I had to get behind the wheel of our car and *watch* my left foot go down on the clutch. My foot knew how to work the clutch, but my head didn't!

All associative learning is trial-and-error learning. When a rat learns to run a maze, it doesn't follow rules, it *practices*. If a trial run fails, no neural connection is wired in; if it succeeds, the brain strengthens that connection. This kind of learning is heavily experience-based. It is also habit-bound—the more times I perform a skill successfully, the more inclined I will be to do it that way the next time. Associative learning is also *tacit* learning—I learn the skill, but I can't articulate any rules by which I learned it and usually I can't even describe how I do it. Neural networks are not connected with our language faculty, nor with our ability to articulate concepts. They are simply embedded in experience. We *feel* our skills, we *do* our skills, but we don't think or talk about them. We develop our skills because they give us a sense of satisfaction or a feeling of reward, or because they help us avoid pain.

A great deal of the knowledge possessed by a corporation is tacit knowledge, knowledge that no one can frame or articulate but upon which the corporation relies for its lifeblood. This tacit knowledge is in the skills and experience of its leaders and employees. An article about the Xerox Corporation in the very first issue of *Fast Company* magazine gave a powerful example of this. Xerox management wanted to cut wasted employee time, so they called in a time-and-motion expert to chart where this waste could be found and eliminated. The expert focused on the coffee machine—engineers, he concluded, spent far too much unnecessary time chatting over cups of coffee. He recommended cuts. Fortunately, Xerox had also hired an anthropologist to accompany the time-and-motion expert.

The anthropologist asked the coffee-loving engineers to show him their repair manuals. At first, they produced their pristine, clean copies, bearing all the official procedures for installing and repairing machines. But as time passed and the engineers came to trust the anthropologist, they showed him their real repair manuals—the ones they actually used when out on a job. These were full of dog-eared pages filled with scribbles of shortcuts and unorthodox procedures that the men had learned by trial and error out on the job. They saved both time and money, and also gave the engineers a glee of satisfaction that they could beat the system. It was these shortcuts and unorthodox procedures that were being exchanged in conversations around the coffee machine.

The upshot of the Xerox study has been an attempt to capitalize on the engineers' tacit skills. The coffee breaks were not shortened, but in addition the company is experimenting with a computerized data bank of tricks learned on the job. Engineers who discover shortcuts that save time and money on official procedures described in the manual have a standing invitation to add their ideas to the data bank. In this way, the company brain gets rewired as the engineers rewire their individual brains.

In recent years, neural network computers (sometimes known as parallel processing computers) have been perfected that can mimic the associative thinking skills of human beings. These computers are used to recognize handwriting, to read postal codes, to discriminate tastes and smells, to "see" faces. And unlike serial processing PCs, neural network computers can learn, they can adapt their programs.

The advantages of associative thinking are that it is in dialogue with experience and can learn through trial and error as it goes along. It can feel its way with untried experience. It constantly rewires the brain. It is also a kind of thinking that can handle nuance and ambiguity—we can remove up to 80 percent of a given pattern, and the brain can still recognize what is left. A neural network computer can recognize a postal code written in millions of different samples of handwriting. The disadvantages of this kind of thinking are that it is slow, inaccurate, and tends to be habit-bound. We *can* relearn a skill, but it takes time and much effort. And because associative thinking is tacit thinking, we have difficulty sharing it with others. We can't just write out a formula and tell another to get on with the job. All of us must learn a skill in our own way, for ourselves. No two brains have the same set of neural connections.

QUANTUM THINKING: THE BRAIN'S "SPIRIT"

The third kind of thinking we can do is creative, insightful, intuitive thinking. It is the kind of thinking with which we challenge our assumptions, break our habits, or change our mental models, our paradigms. It is the kind of thinking that invents new categories of thought, that creates new patterns and new language. This third kind of thinking is also rooted in and motivated by our deep sense of meaning and value. It is our spiritual thinking or our vision thinking. Earlier, in Chapter One, I called it quantum thinking because its capacities and processes are very like those described by quantum physics. And it may very well arise from quantum structures in the brain.

Computers can simulate both serial and associative thinking. PCs do something very like serial thinking faster and more accurately than human beings. Neural network computers can replicate some of our associative thinking abilities, and these machines will certainly get better as their technology develops. But no computer so far built, or even envisaged, can do anything like the creative, insightful thinking at which we excel. Computers work within assumptions, habits, or mental models. They work within rules or programs. They play a finite game. Our quantum thinking moves the goal post. It challenges assumptions and mental models. It *writes* programs, makes and breaks rules. It plays an infinite game.

Quantum thinking is holistic. It unifies and integrates and sees the whole picture. It integrates the thinking processes of the brain's serial and associative systems, and it unifies all the millions of data impinging on the brain at every moment into a field of experience with which we can deal. Quantum thinking itself seems to arise from a field across the brain built up by the synchronized oscillations of neurons from many different parts of the brain. The latest neuroscience knows what is happening in the brain when we do this kind of thinking, but exactly how it happens is still a mystery. Because the operative field is holistic (it cannot be broken down into separate parts), one strong theory is that it is a quantum field.

When I look at a tumbler sitting on a table, a part of my brain responds to its height, another part to its shape, another part to its elliptical rim outline, yet another part to the reflections of light bouncing off it, and so on. Yet the neurons in all these different parts of my brain oscillate at the same frequency, and that is what gives me my perception of the tumbler as a whole—and of its physical context on the table and in the room, and of its meaning to me. Similarly, when I sit at my desk, the 10^{11} different neurons in my brain are being bombarded by countless perceptual data—visual data, tactile data, thermal and auditory data, and the internal data issuing from my thought processes and imagination. There is no central control system in the brain that receives and channels all this data. There is no single "CEO neuron" that manages the lot, nor even an executive committee of neurons. Rather, my whole perceptual field and my whole sense of meaning—my sense of being in the room and knowing why I am there—*self-organizes* itself out of the synchronous oscillations of the various neurons being stimulated.

Creative thinking in business at the team or corporate level—rewiring the team or corporate brain—means that we must have diffuse and flexible infrastructures that can get into a similar sort of synchronous oscillation. In the corporation, we would call it communication. Used properly, Information Technology systems can play a vital role in this, as can the dialogue process discussed in Chapter Eight. The achievement of such corporate synchronicity is the rationale behind Japanese practices of beginning the working day with company songs or group calisthenics. Many schools in the West attempt it with morning assembly.

Quantum thinking has the capacity to question itself and to question the environment. It is called into play when the unexpected happens, in situations of crisis or opportunity when our rule-bound and habit-bound thinking can't cope. If, for instance, we are involved in a training session at Shell's Lensbury Centre in London and a huge Indian elephant suddenly lumbers into the room, crashing down the door as it proceeds, the following sequence of brain events will happen. In the first instance, we will be in a state of shock, not knowing what is happening or what we are seeing. We simply have no existing categories of thought for elephants lumbering into Shell training seminars, no existing neural connections to process such events. Our brains can't handle it.

The brain's first response to the elephant is a desperate attempt to process the data with its existing categories. When this fails, the brain then puts itself on hold. It goes through a thinking process something like, "Wait a minute. I can't make sense of this from where I am starting." The brain then begins to use its quantum thinking processes to rewire itself. It first creates some new perceptual categories that can see the elephant and place it in the context of the room. Then it sets out to create some new meaning categories that can make sense of *why* the elephant is there. Perhaps it escaped from the London zoo and made its way down the Thames to Lensbury. Perhaps a competing oil company wanted to sabotage the Shell training session. Perhaps the instructor arranged for the elephant's arrival to wake up the seminar participants and to illustrate quantum thinking.

The brain tries out each of these possibilities, apparently simultaneously like quantum feelers into the future (virtual transitions), until it arrives at a *story*—a mental model, a new set of neural connections—that makes sense. Having thus rewired itself, the brain is happy with the elephant's presence, even if the participants themselves are not!

All creative thinking is like learning to see the elephant. It is being able to see that existing categories don't work, being able to put those categories on hold, and then being able to create new categories, some of which involve new meaning. It is our ability to do this kind of thinking that makes us truly human, and it arises from the deepest recesses of the self. But using this ability requires that we step outside our usual thinking or usual paradigm. It requires that we gain a further perspective from which we can see the thinking behind our thinking.

Hyperthinking

There is a mathematical theory in modern physics known as *hyperspace*. The gist of this theory is that there are not just three dimensions in space, or even just four, but rather N dimensions, each offering a further perspective on the last. In his excellent 1994 book *Hyperspace*, Michio Kaku uses the example of a family of fish swimming around in a fishbowl. From their perspective, the fish have no sense that they are inside a bowl, or that this bowl is filled with a liquid medium called water. This is just their world and they take it for granted.

But in Kaku's example, one of the fish suddenly takes a big leap that raises him above the surface of the water in his bowl. "Ah," he says, "look where I've come from." He sees the bowl and his fellow fish and the water from this further perspective and he sees that he has come from a world of fishbowls and water. And now he also knows that there is a larger world outside the fishbowl, a medium in which to move other than water. In the parlance of business, he has *recontextualized* his situation.

The first two kinds of thinking, serial and parallel, are themselves already one level of perception above wild instinct. With their aid we can cultivate crops, design houses and factories, write computer programs, and carry out all the other achievements of our technological civilization. They give us some power over nature. But when normal science and technology reach their limits, we have to raise the game to a further level. We have to see the fishbowl within which our thinking is trapped. Such leaps lead to new insight, though even most new insights remain within our basic paradigm—our company's vision statement, its reason for existing, and its style of operation.

To raise beyond the level of existing vision is an experience known only to a few. It is like an experience of death and rebirth, a total transformation of the self or the organization, a true revolution. The "servant leaders" whom I describe in the final chapter of this book are distinguished by their access to this level of revolutionary transformation. Such leaders are skilled at the third kind of thinking, at quantum thinking.

Because thought originates from the brain and then constructs structures and stories in the world, the creations of thought—our thought systems, our philosophies, our organizations, and so on—give us an insight into the nature of thinking. This is very obviously the case in science itself. The Newtonian revolution was the great burst of serial thinking: logical, rational, rule-bound. Eastern thinking and Western prescientific thought were a flowering of the brain's associative, or parallel, thinking abilities: networked, relational, tradition-bound. And quantum physics makes a leap into yet a further perspective. Just as quantum thinking in the brain integrates rational and associative learning structures, quantum physics as a science integrates the insights of mechanistic particle and wave dynamics. Each of these have their counterparts in organizational thinking. Quantum management integrates Western and Eastern management models, Taylorian "Scientific Management," and the softer, more networked "human relations" school.

We can get a better grasp of what quantum thinking is like and how it relates directly to leadership issues by looking at some dramatic contrasts between the Newtonian scientific paradigm and the quantum scientific paradigm, and how each has appeared in a management context. Chapter Three takes up that part of the story.

Eight Principles of the Old and New Science Applied to Leadership

Humanity faces a quantum leap forward. It faces the deepest social upheaval and creative restructuring of all time. Without clearly recognizing it, we are engaged in building a remarkable new civilization from the ground up. . . . This new civilization has its own distinctive outlook; its own ways of dealing with time, space, logic and causality. And, its own principles for the politics of the future.

—Alvin and Heidi Toffler
Creating a New Civilization

The term "Quantum leap" has entered everyday speech from the language of quantum physics. It means not just a big leap, but a leap from one kind of reality to another. In both business and science, it means a leap from a world we understood and could manage to one where at first nothing makes sense. A leap that requires us to rethink our basic categories and strategies, to alter our most cherished and deeply unconscious assumptions. A leap into the unknown—a paradigm shift. The new science of the twentieth century has made such a leap, but not without pain and confusion.

The great Danish physicist Niels Bohr was one of the founding fathers of the new science. He was among the five or six men who conceived the basics of quantum theory. Bohr was a popular public speaker, frequently asked to explain the new science to general audiences. He often began his lectures with a story that he felt expressed the difficulty of such a task.

In Bohr's story, there is a young Jewish religious student who attends three lectures by a famous rabbi. Excited by his experience, the student rushes off to tell his friends about the lectures. The first lecture, he says, was very good—the student had understood every word. The second lecture, though, was even better—very subtle, very profound. The student did not understand this lecture, but the rabbi himself understood every word. The third lecture, however, was the best of all. It was so good that even the rabbi did not understand it!

Bohr himself, he told his audiences, was like the rabbi of the story. He and his fellow scientists had described a new science that was so subtle, so deep, so profound in its implications and so new in its language and concepts that they did not understand what they had done. Nothing in their education or training had prepared them for a new physics that broke all the rules. Schooled in a framework of absolute space and time and iron laws of causality that assured certainty and predictability (and hence control), they were confronted by a quantum world that violated common sense as they knew it. Quantum space and time have little meaning. Quantum events can't be controlled. They happen with no apparent cause, and a quantum *uncertainty* principle replaces the predictable laws of nature with the slippery rules of the gaming house. Bohr called his new science "weird." Einstein said it reminded him of "the system of delusions of an exceedingly intelligent paranoiac, concocted of incoherent elements of thought." He went to his grave trying to prove that it was wrong.

The four new sciences of this century—relativity, quantum mechanics, chaos, and complexity theory—are all different. Each best describes a different level of reality. Relativity is about very large distances and great speeds; quantum mechanics describes the very small world within the atom. Chaos and complexity apply to physical systems on our everyday level of reality, things like the weather, the flow of streams, the beat of the human heart. Yet all these sciences share a common new paradigm. They change the rules of the game in the same way. A great deal of progress has been made this century in understanding the brain, but properly speaking, there is not yet a "new" brain science. Most neuroscientists are still trying to fit their data into the old paradigm.

In the old science, the Newtonian paradigm, nature is seen as simple, law-abiding, and ultimately controllable. The whole science is about organized simplicity. In the new science, the quantum paradigm, nature is seen as complex, chaotic, and uncertain. This science is about learning to live with and to get the fullest potential out of complexity. Attempts at control can be counterproductive.

Newtonian Approach	Quantum Approach
Simple	Complex
Law-abiding	Chaotic
Ultimately controllable	Uncertain

Of all the new sciences, quantum mechanics is generally regarded as the most fundamental. It raises the greatest challenge to our previous ways of thinking. It has also been put to great practical use in the technology that will shape our lives in the next century—superfluids, superconductors, lasers, silicon chips, and, one day soon, quantum computers. The kind of thinking needed to understand quantum mechanics is the key to understanding the whole new paradigm that is emerging in our culture at large. In this chapter, I want to show how quantum thinking helps us to articulate the new paradigm emerging in business. I want to contrast eight key ideas from Newtonian science, and their effects on business thinking, with eight key quantum ideas and their application to new thinking about leadership.

Atomism versus Holism

Old paradigm science, like Greek philosophy before it, is atomistic. This gives us an emphasis on separate working parts, and leads to a tendency toward fragmentation. New paradigm science is holistic. Its emphasis is on relationship, and this leads to a stress on integration.

The ancient Greeks believed that matter could be reduced to its smallest bits. These were called atoms, and the whole universe was thought to consist of four kinds of atoms—earth, air, fire, and water. Newtonian physics kept the idea of atoms, though from the seventeenth century onward scientists realized there were many more kinds. Today we speak of ninety-two kinds of stable atoms, making up the naturally occurring elements.

Atoms are conceived as hard, impenetrable things. One atom cannot get inside another. Each occupies its own place in space and time and cannot be reduced to anything further. Newton suggested the atoms were linked by forces of action and reaction, giving a model of the universe that stresses impact and collision. If the atoms are to avoid collision, they must avoid each other—we call this a controlled situation, or perhaps a "compromise." The familiar desktop toy shown in Figure 3—several steel balls suspended from strings, appropriately called a "Newton's Cradle"—is a good model of the atomistic universe. When any of the steel balls strikes another, it transmits a predictable amount of force to it. The system as a whole seeks to balance these collisions by relaying the force to a ball that is at the end of the line and thus free to move.

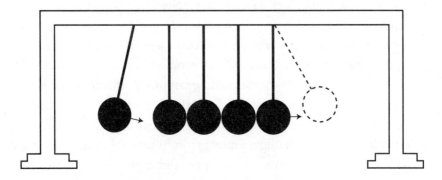

Figure 3. Newton's Cradle

The atomistic model became the basis for the whole modern Western paradigm. Political philosophers like Thomas Hobbes and John Locke used it in their theories of social order. Individuals were conceived as the basic atoms of society, and the institutions and laws of society would be the forces that bound these individuals together, that controlled them. In Locke's liberal individualism, individual needs and individual rights became the focus of attention. The social whole was just the sum of its parts. In the words of a modern Lockian leader, Britain's Margaret Thatcher, "There is no such thing as society. There are just individuals and their families."

Freud used Newton's atomism as the basis for his tragic view of modern psychology. In his "Theory of Object Relations," Freud said that each of us is isolated. He conceived the boundaries of the self as hard and impenetrable. You are an object to me and I just an object to you. We can never really know each other or relate in any fundamental way. I form a picture of you in my own mind, "a projection," and I relate only to that. Love and intimacy are impossible. "The commandment to 'Love thy neighbor as thyself' is the most impossible commandment ever written."

Western medicine, Western education, and Western management have all followed the atomistic model. Doctors are taught to see the body as a collection of separate working parts, and each has its specialist physician. None is taught to see the body as an organic, living whole. Illnesses that seem to weaken the whole system like myeolo-encephalitis (ME) or fatigue or depression are described as "mystery illnesses." We don't really know what causes them, and treatment is at best approximate. Western education divides knowledge into separate subjects and we become expert at some one of them. General, cross-disciplinary education beyond primary school is rare. This kind of education in itself has greatly influenced the kind of leaders we produce. Many of the most inspirational examples of leadership are men and women who dropped out of formal education early, or who followed eccentric educational paths.

Adam Smith's famous pin factory example first introduced the division of labor principle into management. If one worker concentrates on making the heads of pins and another concentrates on the shafts, more pins can be made per day than if each worker makes whole pins. Newtonian organizations are structured into separate areas of expertise, separate divisions, and each of these atomistic units is encouraged to compete with the others. The whole thing is held together by bureaucratic rules and structured hierarchically to impose maximum control from the top. "Transformation" programs are usually piecemeal, directed at improving the efficiency of some function or division. There is little emphasis on teamwork.

The great twentieth-century quantum physicist David Bohm described atomism as "the virus of fragmentation." "For fragmentation is now very widespread," he said, "not only throughout society, but also in each individual; and this is leading to a kind of general confusion of the mind, which creates an endless series of problems and interferes with our clarity of perception so seriously as to prevent us from being able to solve most of them. . . . The notion that all these fragments are separately existent is evidently an illusion, and this illusion cannot do other than lead to endless confusion and conflict."

Quantum physics teaches that the world does not consist of any kind of separate, solid things. At the most fundamental level of reality, physical systems consist of patterns of dynamic energy. Bohm writes that the whole universe consists of interacting, overlapping patterns of dynamic energy that criss-cross and "interfere" in a "pattern of unbroken wholeness." Each quantum "bit" has a particle-like aspect, an aspect that can be pinned down, measured, located in space and time. But it also has a wavelike aspect, vibrations of further potentiality that, in principle, reach all the way across the universe. The future possibilities, and even the future identity, of each bit are internally bound up with the possibilities and identities of all the others. No one bit can be abstracted out and viewed on its own without loss or distortion.

The ambiguous and heavily relational boundaries of quantum entities are known as "contextualism." To be known, to be measured, to be used, a quantum entity must always be seen within the larger context of its defining relationships. Change the context, and the entity itself is different. It realizes another of its infinite potentialities. It *becomes* something different. Something more.

Old Paradigm		New Paradigm
Atomism	versus	Holism
Emphasis on separate working parts	versus	Emphasis on relationship
Fragmentation	versus	Integration

The atomistic Newtonian organization sees itself isolated in its environment, and sees its divisions and employees isolated within its own mechanistic system. Such organizations seek to control both their employees and their environment.

The holistic "quantum organization" would be more sensitive to its context, internal and external. It would be aware, to paraphrase the famous words of the eighteenth-century poet John Donne, that no organization is an island.

At Motorola, as we have seen, the envisaged twenty-year transformation process is meant to embrace every employee in the company, from janitors, telephonists, and secretaries to the CEO himself. A company-wide dialogue process including every individual is integral to this program. Motorola University has a "Culture and Technology" section devoted to monitoring the impact of Motorola products, such as mobile phones, on emerging societies, like newly modernizing China. Within Marks & Spencer, (M&S) global buying trips are made by cross-departmental, cross-specialist teams. In-store merchandise displays located in specialist departments feature goods available throughout each store. Such holistic strategies are in response to customers' perceived desire to mix and match across departments. M&S has a team working in every developing country to monitor local political, social, and economic sensitivities. The company also maintains a practice with small, local suppliers to ensure that a supplier accustomed to orders of $1 million a year who suddenly does a $3 million turnover because of M&S purchases doesn't then go out of business if orders return to normal. "We don't want to be in the business of ruining other people's businesses," says Joint Managing Director Andrew Stone. "We flourish when every part or partner flourishes. If those who supply us benefit in pay and conditions by making goods that please our customers, everybody wins. We even get on with our competition. They bring customers to a shopping center in which we trade, and they benefit from the 'traffic' we create!"

Holistic leadership recognizes that customer needs and expectations, economic and political context, aspirations and strategies of other companies, local and global ecological situations are all part of the organization's internal being and potentiality. Such relational factors will certainly affect results. They should affect strategies. Competitor companies are also among an organization's customers and suppliers. Employees and junior managers are an organization's intellectual capital. As the modern playwright Arthur Miller said, "The fish is in the water, but the water is also in the fish." Both fish and water must be healthy. They are in a symbiotic balance.

The quantum organization would seek to build infrastructures that reach into and integrate the environment, infrastructures that can cooperate with the environment and cocreate a new reality for both. The ethos of cooperation and integration is very different from the ethos of control.

Determinate versus Indeterminate

Old paradigm science is determinate. Iron laws govern all the movements of particles and larger bodies. It values certainty and predictability. New paradigm science is indeterminate. Predictability and control are impossible, even damaging. Quantum and chaotic systems thrive on uncertainty and ambiguity.

The Western mind has always looked for the causes of events, explanations that would put experience within a workable framework. In ancient and medieval times, explanations were sought in the whims or anger of the gods, punishment for human sin, or the movements of the stars. None of these lay within human control. Newtonian science introduced a new kind of causality. Everything in the physical world happens, Newton said, because it *has* to happen. The whole universe is governed by three simple laws of motion and the universal law of gravitation. The universe is like a giant clockwork machine that God set in motion to run for the rest of time. B will always follow A in the same way if the starting position and the forces acting upon A are the same. If we know these facts about any physical situation, we can predict its outcome without fail. Knowledge means control.

In an age when human beings felt like helpless pawns in the face of unpredictable natural catastrophe, Newtonian determinism caught the general imagination. It was the new panacea, the final explanation for all mysteries. It gave rise to a faith in technique, to the great conquests of technology and to instrumental reason—the kind of reason that asks, What is the best way to do x?

Freud, who saw himself as the Newton of the mind, imported determinism into his new "scientific psychology." In his "hydraulic model" of the self, we are divided into three compartments—the id, the ego, and the superego. The id is the basement of the self, the dark, instinctive forces of sex and aggression. The superego is the overwhelming forces of parental and societal expectations. The poor ego, the conscious self, is sandwiched between the two, pushed helplessly around from below and pressured into guilt from above. Our feelings and behavior throughout life are fully determined by these conflicting forces and the experience of our first five years.

The legal system took up Freud's determinism with its notion of the "guilty victim"—the criminal forced into crime because of an unhappy childhood, a deprived neighborhood environment, or an abusive school. Behavioral psychology described human beings as so many Pavlovian dogs, determined to act with a fixed response to any given stimulus. More recently still, artificial intelligence (AI) has told us that we are all just ambulatory computers, programmed for success or failure. Genetic scientists say that behavior patterns like addiction, criminality, and sexual orientation are programmed in our genes.

Where Newton looked for the laws of the universe and Freud the laws and dynamics of the psyche, Frederick Taylor's Scientific Management looked for the laws inherent within each organization. Find those laws, understand the machinery of the organization, and a leader can exercise control. Most senior managers in our Newtonian organizations value control above all else—control over their subordinates, control over the products, control over the market and customer desire. They plan against contingency and seek answers to questions before they arise. I saw a postcard in one executive's office that read "Control the unexpected."

There is a theorem in cybernetic theory, the science that tries to bridge the living and machine worlds, that points out the limitations of too much control. Known as Von Foerster's Theorem, it says:

> The more rigidly connected are the elements of a system, the less influence they will have on the system as a whole. The more rigid the connections, the more each element of the system will exhibit a greater degree of "alienation" from the whole.

The more controlled the parts of a system, the less they contribute to the system and the less they are part of the whole. The new science helps us to understand why this is so.

Quantum physics is radically indeterminate. Quantum events just happen as they happen, without rhyme or reason, making the prediction of any one event impossible. We can never know when any given radioactive atom will decay, nor which path an excited subatomic particle will follow in getting from A to B. Quantum bits emerge into existence out of nowhere and disappear again just as mysteriously. What is more, this indeterminism is vital to the creative holism of quantum systems.

It is precisely because the identity, the coordinates, and the possible movements of individual quantum entities are ambiguous that a whole quantum system can "fall into place," all its constituent elements integrally interrelated and working for the greater good (the eventual stability or creativity) of both themselves and the system. Because they are indeterminate, quantum entities *have no fully fixed identity* until they are in relationship. This gives the quantum system maximum flexibility to define itself as it goes along. It cocreates with its environment. All of nature's complex systems are at their most creative when they are delicately poised between fixedness and unfixedness—poised at the edge of chaos.

Andrew Stone of Marks & Spencer says that understanding the dynamics of quantum and complex systems has changed the way he manages. I saw one striking instance of this recently in the way he conducted a meeting of his directors. Marks & Spencer was developing a global procurement policy to supply its growing international retail sales. Stone felt such a policy needed to be written up, and he drafted a vague outline of one. When he presented this to his twelve colleagues, they said, "This is a wonderful idea, Andrew. But it's not yet practice. How do we do it?" In reply, Stone threw up his hands and said, "Don't ask me. You know I have too many ideas and never know how to put them into practice. You are great at implementing!" After moments of stunned silence followed by embarrassed guffaws, the room broke into an excited free-for-all of suggestions, plans, and schemes. Everyone had an idea. The ambiguity of Stone's approach had released the creativity of those who worked with him. When a plan does emerge, it will belong to the group as a whole, rather than being a policy imposed upon them. Such an approach challenges the simplistic truth of the old dictum that "It is the business of leaders to lead."

Indeterminacy and ambiguity also play a significant role in the style used by many Asian managers. I have been working with a group of Japanese and Korean businesspeople for over a year to set up a research institute. Time and again they give me itineraries and state their intentions, then when I have followed through by setting up appointments for them or clearing some red tape they telephone at the last minute and say, "We have changed our plans." When I ask in the best Western style, "So when are you coming? What is going to happen next?" they respond, "We don't know." The vagueness continues for months while they maintain maximum flexibility. Then very suddenly, and with stunning effect, some key venture falls into place. Their way. While I have been tormented by their dithering and ambiguity, they have been keeping large numbers of indeterminate balls in the air until just the right (best for them!) situation emerges. Such stories of protracted and frustrating contract negotiations between Eastern and Western companies are rife. The competitive advantage usually rests with the party best able to handle and use the ambiguity.

Leading chaos and maximizing creativity requires learning to thrive on ambiguity. Quantum leadership implies that control give way to some more subtle, intuitive feel for the situation and the creative potential of its indeterminacy. The infrastructures and strategies of the quantum organization would themselves have to be designed to allow for ambiguity and indeterminacy. This in turn requires that the quantum leader find new reliance on trust—trust in the leader's own character and intuition, trust in the character, intuition, and abilities of subordinates, and trust in the dynamics of the organization. And it requires trust in the emergent potential of "self-organization," nature's own most creative response to chaos. We can look at this next.

Old Paradigm		New Paradigm
Determinate	versus	Indeterminate
Value certainty and predictability	versus	Thrive on uncertainty and ambiguity
Control	versus	Trust

Reductive versus Emergent and Self-Organizing

In Newtonian science, reduction and analysis are key. Any system or object is reduced to its parts. The parts are isolated and analyzed for ultimate properties or primary function. The whole is considered to be the sum of its parts, so we best know the whole by knowing those parts. This is hands-on science—grab the system, tear it to pieces, learn how to control the parts, gain power over the whole.

The division of labor is a reductive philosophy. Break the job into parts and do it more efficiently. Breaking organizations into competing divisions is reductive. Each division, it is argued, can be most effective concentrating on its own region of focus.

Newtonian parts are whatever they are, wherever we find them or in whatever combination. Adding A and B together just gives us A + B. A gear is the same gear and has the same function whether it is part of a lawnmower, a car, or a spaceship. Newtonian organizations tend to carry on regardless of their environments, each division going its own way, each employee following a separate job description. Such organizations are broken down and viewed in isolation from their environments with a view to maximizing control. How else could a five-year plan be inviolate except in such a vacuum? Some control is necessary, of course. But how much?

In new paradigm science, emergence and self-organization are key. Quantum wholes are *larger* than the sum of their parts. A quantum system has additional properties and potential not possessed individually by the parts. And both the parts and the whole system are contextual, context-dependent. A quantum bit is one thing in one environment, quite a different thing in another environment. Because each bit has both individual (particle-like) and system (wavelike) properties, the system properties only develop within a system, within a context. They *emerge* within the context. Thus we can never identify the nature, properties, or potential of a quantum thing without knowing its wider context. In leading quantum organizations, the leader's purposes themselves emerge in a wider context.

Existing systems theory talks a great deal about the need to see things in larger context. But nonetheless it remains mechanistic because it is atomistic. The parts of systems described by systems theory are not themselves contextual. They don't change *internally* through different relationships. They remain unchanging black boxes. This is one way in which quantum thinking and quantum contextualism require some radical rethinking by systems theorists.

If we try to pin down a quantum thing and isolate it from its environment, we *reduce* it. (The technical quantum term is to say that its wave function collapses. Many complex possibilities become one simple actuality.) Thus trying to control the uncertain system properties of the thing destroys those very properties. Tight control is achieved at the expense of lost potential. Fullest potential is achieved by letting the system unfold, emerge, as it will. No amount of controlled intervention can foresee and realize emergent possibilities. They just happen as they happen, in dialogue with the system's wider environment.

Similarly, the intricate properties of complex systems emerge at the edge of chaos. Such systems self-organize—no kind of technique (control) can put them together. They have an unanalyzable, holistic dynamic of their own. The Frankenstein myth is all about the folly of trying to put a human being together out of bodily parts. Many a Newtonian organization has created a bureaucratic Frankenstein's monster with its emphasis on top-down control, tight structure, and imposed plans or solutions, and its obsession with efficiency. Like the creature in Shelley's novel, such organizations have their own way of getting out of control.

Old Paradigm		New Paradigm
Reductive	versus	Emergent
Isolated and Controlled	versus	Contextual and Self-Organizing
The parts completely define the whole	versus	The whole is greater than the sum of its parts
Top-Down Management	versus	Bottom-Up Leadership
Reactive	versus	Imaginative and Experimental

The whole shift in management thinking today is toward the networked or knowledge-based organization. Knowledge (as opposed to mere information) is always contextual. The wider the context in which our knowledge operates, the more meaning it takes on and the more leverage it affords. There is also a growing realization that organizations—or divisions within organizations—cannot be isolated from their wider environments. That fish-and-water insight again. Just as in quantum and chaotic physical systems, the futures of creative human organizations can only emerge in a free-flowing (that is, not heavily controlled) dialogue with the wider economic, political, social, and ecological environments. This again requires a new kind of trust, a trust in the emergent properties of complex situations. And trust requires infrastructures where emergence can unfold, infrastructures that allow the organization to tap into its own collective intelligence, that part of itself that is larger than the sum of its parts. I will discuss this in connection with dialogue structures later on.

Either-Or versus Both-And

Old paradigm science is a science of either-or. Founding itself on Aristotle's logic, which argued that a statement is either true or false, Newtonian science argues that something is a wave or a particle; a particle is here or there, now or then. Newtonian physical systems are linear. They follow one smooth path from A to B. We all learned in high school geometry that the shortest path from A to B is a straight line.

Either-or logic and linearity are part of the whole Western paradigm. Historians of science feel it is no accident that modern science arose first in the monotheistic countries of the West. We are the culture of one truth, one God, one way. We admire a leader who "knows her own mind" or "keeps his eye on the ball" and sees clearly one vision to pursue. We applaud a young student or athlete who sets out on career preparation with "single-minded dedication." In education, in politics, in military strategy, and in business we seek to find that one best way to do things. We debate about it, we go to war over it, we kill people for it. In his Scientific Management theory, Frederick Taylor argued that there is always one best strategy for any company to pursue. The whole point of discussions, brainstorming sessions, and strategy meetings is to find that best strategy and then to pursue it ruthlessly.

Clearly, there are times when decisiveness and certainty about the best way forward are an advantage. In our goal-oriented, problem-solving culture, it seems the only advantage. Yet we all know that there is a downside to too much single-mindedness and certainty too early on. We speak of "blinkered idealism" and people who "can't see the woods for the trees." There are metaphors about horses that "get the bit between their teeth." Common sense tells us there are times when caution, open-mindedness, or even a little bit of healthy uncertainty may be more appropriate, but there is little in the philosophy of Western culture, Western science, or Western management to support these qualities.

In our Newtonian organizations, both political and corporate, there is a constant and seemingly unresolvable tension between the individual (the particle) and the group (the wave). How do we foster the initiative and creative qualities of the individual while at the same time developing the cooperation and team qualities of the group? Western liberal individualism is atomistic. It stresses the crucial importance of the individual and is suspicious of the group. The eighteenth-century French philosopher Jean-Jacques Rousseau, like Karl Marx after him, saw the advantages of the group, or the collective. Both were suspicious of individuals and wanted to limit their rights. Asian countries often have dreadful human rights records and limited individual creativity, but their capacity to work on teams, to dedicate themselves to the common good, and to tap into a kind of collective energy and intelligence often puts the West to shame. It is a significant competitive advantage for some Asian industries.

The new science of the twentieth century is radically different from the either-or paradigm. Quantum entities are both particle-like and wavelike at the same time. They are both point sources of action situated precisely in this place in space and this moment in time and wavelike fingers of potentiality present everywhere in space and time simultaneously, interconnected members of other systems. The particle-like aspect is the hereness and nowness of the entity—its actuality. But the wavelike aspect represents all its future possibility. In quantum systems, we saw, relationship creates further possibility. A quantum whole C is larger than the sum of its parts A + B. Each quantum "individual" has a *further* group potentiality. A quantum organization would seek to capitalize on this insight. It would build infrastructures that bypass the old individual-versus-group dichotomy, infrastructures that allow individuals to flourish both as individuals and as members of larger creative groups. A quantum leader would cultivate his or her own inner light and individual potential, but at the same time be always aware that a truly creative leader draws a great deal of insight and inspiration from the unexpressed qualities of the group being led. Such leadership would not be wholly top-down control, but at least partly bottom-up learning, sensing the emergent and self-organizing possibilities of the group.

> A quantum leader would cultivate his or her own inner light and individual potential, but at the same time be always aware that a truly creative leader draws a great deal of insight and inspiration from the unexpressed qualities of the group being led.

There is a famous character in quantum lore who expresses the both-and nature of quantum reality. This is Schrödinger's Cat, the mascot of the new science. Schrödinger's Cat has been put into an opaque box along with a fiendish device, a radioactive source that can trigger the release of either food or poison. (See Figure 4.) Common sense would tell us that if the device releases food the cat will live, and if it releases poison the cat will die. But radioactive sources are quantum devices, and Schrödinger's Cat is a quantum cat, existing separately and simultaneously in several places. So the device releases *both* food *and* poison, and the cat is *both* alive *and* dead. (Until we look at it, but I'll keep that part of the story for a later time.)

The story of the quantum cat is also a metaphor for the way that quantum systems evolve. When a quantum bit wants to get from A to B, it doesn't follow just one path. On the contrary, it throws out an infinite number of possible paths—these are called *virtual transitions*. Each path represents one possibly best path from A to B, a "feeler toward the future." In fact, in quantum reality, B itself is not yet sharply defined. B is still part of a future scenario yet to emerge. So infinite possible paths strike out from A toward an uncertain or ambiguous B, mutually defining the future as they interfere with (get into dialogue with) each other. This allows the whole system to be creative in responding to its own uncertain future. In the end, B will emerge, and one of the infinite paths from A to B will emerge as the "right path."

Inside the box, unobserved, Schrödinger's cat is both alive *and* dead.

If we open the box and *look*, the cat is dead.

Figure 4.   Schrödinger's Cat

A quantum system's many paths from A to B remind me of the ethos behind Shell Oil's "scenario planning." Scenario planning is a strategy device that gets leaders to imagine many possible futures for a given situation and then in turn to imagine the best strategy for handling each. This way, it is assumed, Shell will be ready with an action plan for any eventuality. The strategy worked brilliantly in the 1970s oil crisis. One of Shell's scenarios was that the Arab countries would turn off the taps. Shell was the only oil company that had a contingency plan ready for this "impossible" situation. It made a profit; the other companies lost heavily.

When an organization settles on "one best path" from A to B, it commits all its resources and energy to a strategy that may not be best, that may even be a mistake. When it sets a tightly defined B as its goal, that B is the best it will ever get. Quantum systems are creative precisely because they play on the uncertainty of both means and ends. Infrastructures that allow an organization to do the same would greatly contribute to its creative flexibility and to its ability to thrive on external uncertainty.

Both quantum and chaotic systems are nonlinear. Quantum systems evolve in quantum leaps, radical jumps from one definite state to another with nothing but feelers of potentiality in between. Chaotic systems can be massively perturbed by the slightest input. In linear systems, a large effect requires a large cause. Small causes have almost no effects. The famous "butterfly effect" shows how this is untrue for nonlinear, chaotic systems. The implication of both quantum and chaos sciences is that no input or disturbance is so small that it can be safely overlooked. No part of a system is insignificant. Production engineers have found to their horror that the very slightest defect in one small part can escalate to disturb a whole manufacturing process. Consultants working with companies have commented on their surprise to find how much the janitors and tea ladies, never mind the secretaries, know—expertise that is overlooked because it is thought insignificant.

Both quantum feelers toward the future and chaotic nonlinearity remind me of the human imagination and of children's play. In our imaginations, we do not restrict ourselves to one possible scenario. Sometimes we imagine three or four different outcomes or activities simultaneously. That is why imagination is part of the creative process. When children play, they seldom have a fixed goal nor are they much bothered about the reality of their dramas. They throw out experiments in every direction, and are thus much more creative than adults. As adults, we lose our capacity for play. We fear the make-believe and replace it with the definite goal, the practical solution. In our schools, we teach children to *concentrate,* to narrow down the options and focus on definite learning goals (usually exams). In our organizations, we expect employees and managers to "focus on the job." We like directors to come to meetings with plans, reports, and vision statements.

I recently attended a meeting of the global team handling Marks & Spencer's women's fashions division. Five divisional directors attended, along with Andrew Stone, their managing director. The meeting was opened by one divisional director saying that none had brought formal reports. "We know," he said to Stone, "that you don't like these. Instead, we'll just throw out a few ideas and try to share our excitement about some new product lines." For two hours the four men and one woman spoke of the possibilities they imagined. They passed model bras around the table, proudly displayed new shirts, and tried on foolish-looking hats. They were like children playing with objects drawn out of a treasure chest, enjoying themselves and what they were doing. Their sense of fun was palpable. The women's fashions division is Marks & Spencer's *most* profitable division. The creative play at its source successfully excites the market.

Body language, styles of dress, tones of voice, personal taste, metaphors—these are all part of our ambiguous and playful communication. Each carries several messages simultaneously and facilitates the unfolding of emergent meaning and possibility in a strategy meeting. Such richness is lost in an e-mail communication, a crisp fax, or the deadpan tone of a director's formal report. It is lost whenever people in meetings are formal and stiff. Leaders who lead with heavy top-down authority or fear lose the playful potential of those whom they would lead. They lose their *own* playful potential.

Heisenberg's Uncertainty Principle

The executive director of men's wear at Marks & Spencer opened a senior strategy meeting to discuss revising the global code of ethics by saying, "It's really good we're confused about this. If we thought we knew what we're doing here we'd cock it up. We need some uncertainty to give us room to think." This man, in his late fifties and with little formal education, had probably never given the new science a thought. But his leadership style went straight to the heart of quantum thinking.

Mechanistic science was about *knowing*. Its style of knowing depended upon isolating elements of systems and focusing on them. Its central achievement was a gloating promise to have delivered answers to all nature's questions. At the end of the nineteenth century, Lord Kelvin, the president of Britain's prestigious science academy, the Royal Society, advised his best graduate students to avoid physics as a career. "We've solved all the problems there," he said. "There is nothing left to discover." The old management culture, like the old science that inspired it, relied on a quest for focus, certainty, and control. It stood to reason, according to the popular wisdom of that culture, that the more a leader knew about a situation and the more tightly he could structure any possible contingencies, the better the outcome he would achieve. Mechanistic managers like answers, things they can manage (the Latin root of manage is *manus,* the word for hand, the root of hands-on).

The most important principle of the new science focuses our attention on the importance of *not knowing* everything about a situation. Indeed, on the impossibility of knowing everything. According to Heisenberg's Uncertainty Principle, those who would create structures, design strategies, or make decisions are forever destined to grasp at shadows in the fog—and a good thing it is too!

In quantum science, the constantly shifting and contextual properties of things come in pairs of "complementary variables." So a particle moving through space will have position and momentum variables, it will have x and y variables, z and z' variables, and so on. But the Uncertainty Principle tells us we can only know one member of a pair of complementary variables at a time. If we set out to measure the position of a particle, for instance, its momentum will become fuzzy and indeterminate. Alternatively, we can choose to measure the momentum if we wish, but then the position will elude our grasp. We can never know both position and momentum. This has enormous implications in both science and business.

The first big implication of the Uncertainty Principle is that the questions we ask in any situation determine the answers we get. And the answers we don't get. Whenever we interfere with a quantum system—by questioning it, by measuring it, by focusing on it—we pluck out one aspect of the system from the many-possibilitied whole, and we lose all the other associated possibilities. We see only what we look for.

Light, for instance, has the possibility to be both particle-like and wavelike, but as with Schrödinger's Cat, we can never catch it in its double act. With the cat, when we open its box it is *either* alive *or* dead; with light, when we measure it, it is *either* particle-like *or* wavelike. If a scientist asks a particle-like question, that is, designs an experiment in which a beam of light is measured with a particle detector (a photo-multiplier tube), the light will hit the detector as a stream of particles. If, on the other hand, the scientist asks a wavelike question by measuring the light with a wave detector (a screen), the light will hit the detector as a wavelike interference pattern. This experiment, known as the Two-Slit Experiment, is the most famous in quantum science. (See Figure 5.)

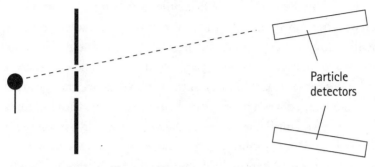

If you observe a photon with a particle detector, you get a particle.

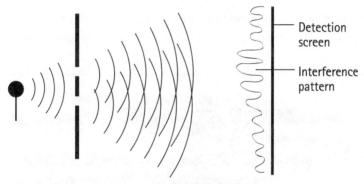

If you observe a photon with a wave detector, you get a wave.

Figure 5.   Two-Slit Experiment

Similarly, a corporate recruitment officer might ask a prospective employee a series of "particle-like" questions. How old are you? What is your employment history? Your marital status? Your educational background? And so on. Such questions will produce a lot of facts that the recruitment officer can write in a report, but when the prospective employee leaves the room, the officer will have precious little idea about the kind of person who just walked out. If, on the other hand, the recruitment officer uses a more "wavelike" approach, simply spending time with the prospective employee, chatting, exploring personal interests, perhaps lunching together, the session will generate a strong sense of the interviewee as a person—but very few facts.

A senior member of Peter Chadwick Ltd., one of Europe's exciting young consultancy firms, expressed how his team is in danger of being caught out by the Uncertainty Principle. Referring to the corporate fixation with bottom-line results and how this affects the way consultants lead clients through change processes, he said, "As consultants, we know that we cost a lot of money, so we just *assume* that we should deliver our clients big monetary savings as a net result. If, however, we thought that what the client wanted was a fundamental culture change, with less immediate emphasis on quantifiable, short-term gains, we would use a very different approach and put a wholly different change process into play." The assumptions consultants make determine the results they will get for their clients. Different assumptions would mean different results.

Any time we act on a quantum system, we change it. Our questions, our assumptions, our prejudices, our beliefs—in short, our paradigm— determine how we will act, and therefore what changes we will bring about.

Heisenberg's Uncertainty Principle
"We can focus on the position or on the momentum of a particle, but never on both."

- When we focus on one aspect of a situation, we abstract that aspect out from the whole, and we lose its associated possibilities.

- When we interfere with a quantum system, we change it.

The second big implication of the Uncertainty Principle is the message it gives us about structure, about how tightly it is wise to structure situations and our approach to systems. In the laboratory, the scientist's experimental design provides the structure for the activity. But it also dictates the outcome of his experiment, as in the Two-Slit Experiment with light. The particle-detecting structure dictated that light would show itself as a stream of particles. It can be the same in business, sometimes with disastrous results.

During the course of one two-day session I spent with a group of senior Peter Chadwick operations managers, the theme of structure arose time and again. Initially, the team believed that structure was essential both to their consultancy work with clients and to their own company identity. "If we didn't have structure," asked one member, "what would happen to the identity of 'Peter Chadwick'?" By structure here, he meant a standardized methodology for dealing with clients, a recognizable style of approach, a curriculum for training new members of the company, and so on. Another team member voiced the shared view that a consultant's main job with a client company was "to go in and implement new systems and processes." That is, give the company a formula for how to improve. This formula is arrived at by the consultant during the period of analysis, the initial period of breaking the client company's problems down into their constituent pieces and then drafting a project goal. Analysis—> Project Goal—> Implementation Plans = Go In and Do It.

"The trouble with this," one of the Peter Chadwick managers recalled during our discussion, "is that it can go badly wrong. The CEO's focus may be wrong. I remember one case where we accepted a Project Goal with a company. The Project Goal succeeded beyond all expectation. But the company failed to realize the expected financial benefit. Its original focus had been too fragmentary."

A project goal is a structure. According to the Uncertainty Principle, any structure results in outcomes that preclude other outcomes. By the end of our two-day session, the Peter Chadwick team members came deeply to question their initial reliance on structure. A three-hour dialogue session focused on the identity of the company had not raised one mention of structure. Rather, the group decided the company's real identity lay "in the way we think, and in our energy." As for imposing structures on clients, they came round to realizing the real success of their young company rested more on a spirit of cocreativity with those clients. Listening to the clients, feeling their way forward toward various possibilities in dialogue with the clients, *feeling* the situation in which they were being asked to intervene. None of this had anything to do with structure. On the contrary, tight structure would have made this style of consultancy impossible.

A business consultant is one kind of "servant leader." I will discuss the servant leader at great length at the end of this book, but just in passing here it is important to say that such leaders lead from within. They lead with listening, with intuition, with gut feeling, and they lead in service to a deeper vision than either they or those whom they lead can at first articulate. Such leadership requires a high tolerance for uncertainty, for ambiguity, and for loose structure that allows the dynamics of a situation to play itself through. Heisenberg's Uncertainty Principle, and its larger implications, sums all this up. At some point, any leader must make decisions, must impose structure and put strategies into play. But to do so with an awareness of cost is to do so in a different way and with a different sense of timing. As the Marks & Spencer director said, "We need some uncertainty to give us room to think."

Actuality versus Potentiality

Old paradigm science is concerned with the "here and now," with things it can see and touch and measure. Its focus is on actuality. The new science has discovered that much that is interesting or valuable about physical systems lies hidden, is beyond our grasp, or is yet to unfold.

This potentiality aspect of the new science is perhaps the most difficult for people in our culture to grasp. Facts are, after all, facts. Let's stick to them. A bird in the hand is worth two in the bush. If you are a Newtonian scientist, you trust what is before your eyes. You trust substances that you can capture in test tubes, subject to analysis, and describe on graphs bordered by Cartesian coordinates. Likewise, as a Newtonian manager, you trust quarterly returns, solid figures you can send to your stockholders. You trust results. You know an employee is busy when you can *see* papers shuffle and hands move, when you can measure the number of hours the employee has spent at the desk.

We know from the latest brain science—and, if we reflect on it, from our own experience—that we do our most creative thinking when the mind is not busy. When we concentrate on a particular mental task, the mind focuses the bulk of its energy on that task. This is effective for achieving the goal in sight, but it fragments the unity of our consciousness. We make fewer sideways (lateral) associations. The mind cannot extend down into the deep pool of unitary consciousness from which things are seen in a broader perspective. These associations and broader perspectives emerge only when we take our minds off some particular task. When we relax, when we sleep, when we get up from our desks and walk down the hall to the coffee pot, this is when we suddenly see the whole picture, when things fall into place. Many of us have had the experience of solving a problem by sleeping on it. This is because during sleep the mind reunifies itself. Awareness makes contact with the ground state, or full potentiality, of consciousness. If, at work, we feel we must always be seen to be busy, then we are not allowing our minds to tap into that vast pool of creative potentiality.

In quantum science, as we saw, any attempt to grab hold of and measure a system collapses all the manifold potentiality of the system into one actuality. Heisenberg's Uncertainty Principle told us that anything we can say about a quantum system is only a part of the story. Facts aren't always just facts. Understanding depends upon how we look at facts, upon what questions we have asked in arriving at them. Birds in the hand are all very well, but in grabbing any one of them we destroy the pattern of the whole flock. Sometimes that pattern might have contained information or beauty of value to us.

Sometimes metaphors are the most powerful way to understand difficult concepts. In his book *Finite and Infinite Games,* James Carse has arrived at the perfect metaphor for expressing what business needs to understand about actuality versus potentiality. Actuality, the here and now that is in front of our eyes, is the stuff of what Carse calls a "finite game." "Finite games," he says, "are played for the purpose of winning. They are played *within* boundaries." Leaders who go for bottom-line results, companies that measure share value in terms of tangible assets or that invest their research budgets in technology for the given, are playing a finite game. When Shell describes itself as "an oil company," it is playing a finite game. When consultants narrow their task to doing what the client wants, to pleasing the client, they are playing a finite game. And when health care systems invest endless funds in interventive medicine to cure illness, they are playing a finite game. All finite games have in common the acceptance of a limited playing field.

Potentiality—that unlimited pool of infinite, unfolding possibility, those things on which we can't yet quite focus, that won't neatly fit into boxes—is the stuff of what Carse calls an "infinite game." "Infinite play-ers," he says, "play for the purpose of continuing play. Infinite games play *with* boundaries." A leader who goes for growth instead of immediate bottom-line returns is playing an infinite game. A company that finds some way to measure the value of its *intangible* assets—its software, the creativity of its people, the power of its deep vision—and that invests a good portion of its research funds into research for the unknown is also playing an infinite game. When consultants place what the client wants in the larger context of what the client needs, they are playing an infinite game. And when health care systems invest less in the never-ending cost of interventive medicine for illness and more in quality-of-life support for health, they are playing an infinite game. All infinite games have in com-mon that they are played on an unlimited field. They are sustainable.

Subject–Object Split versus Participatory Universe

Old paradigm science divides the world into subjects and objects. The sci-entist is detached from the environment. The world is "out there." New paradigm science is participatory. The subject (the scientist) is "in the world," where involvement helps to make the world happen.

Western culture has always been dualistic. It divides the world into subjects and objects, minds and bodies, spirit and matter. The Newton-ian universe is a material universe, made of cold, brute matter that simply is as it is. Newtonian scientists are detached observers who look at their world, weigh and measure it, and do experiments on it. They stand back from nature and study it. Newtonian technologists use nature, they manipulate and control it.

Newtonian organizations divide the world into the organization and its environment, the organization and its market. They seek to manage (control) that environment and to exploit the market. Natural resources are just that, resources to be used. Customers are out there and they too are to be managed. Their tastes are to be manipulated, their dissatisfac-tions stoked up, their expectations set. Such organizations make a sharp division between management and labor, between those who make deci-sions and those who are expected to follow them passively or to react through their official agents. As the senior manager of one global elec-tronics plant reminded me, "It is the business of management to manage and of unions to react"—like Newtonian billiard balls bashing into one another. God forbid they should, as I had suggested to him, sit down and dialogue with each other. At an American communications company, employees are described as "most valued resources"; at a Swedish financial services company they are "intellectual capital." Such mechanistic language reinforces mechanistic behavior and learning structures.

In Western liberal democracies, we make a sharp split between the public and the private. This follows from our Western concept of the self, as I shall discuss later. In our Newtonian organizations, this split underlies a sharp division between the world of work and the employee's conduct at work, and the world of private life. Newtonian employees (including managers) bring to work only those aspects of themselves deemed directly relevant to the job, those aspects that have to do with dealing efficiently with the job, fulfilling the clauses of the contract under which they were hired, aligning themselves with the goals, values, and concerns of the company. They relate to their superiors, subordinates, and colleagues with these goals in mind. Anything else belongs to private life and is no concern of the organization for which the employee works. This *anything else* includes personal relationships and their accompanying joys and sorrows, children's needs and illnesses, outside passions and interests, personal idiosyncrasies, personal pain. The very modern Newtonian organization has a counseling service where such things can be discussed, if necessary (and in private), so they cause less distraction to the employee's work effectiveness.

A senior manager at Shell Oil told me, "When I am at home for the weekend with my family, we go for walks in the country. We talk to each other, we meet with our friends. I love my children, I care about nature. But when I go to work on Monday morning, I am expected to leave all that outside the door. My job is about making money." Yet this man's actual job is in the human resources division of his company. He describes loneliness as his greatest problem at work. He feels that he can't give all of himself to his job.

A senior member of the Peter Chadwick managerial team returned from a three-week holiday with his family. "I realized," he said, "that we have all the priorities wrong and this is damaging. We focus only on the quality of work, not on the quality of life. But now I realize that if you focus more on quality of life, you improve the quality of work." A Newtonian organization does not make room for these insights. An employee's quality of life is a private concern.

In new paradigm science, it is impossible for observers to distance themselves from what they observe. Both are mutually codefined parts of the same holistic system. The questions quantum scientists ask, the experimental apparatus they design, play an *active, cocreative* role in the result that emerges. We saw this with the Two-Slit Experiment about light. A "particle question" evokes particles, a "wave question" evokes waves. Reality is not something out there but rather a constantly evolving drama in which human beings are partners.

The common Newtonian notion that organizations or those who lead them simply act upon or react to their surroundings is an illusion, an illusion with crippling effect. In the words of Fons Trompenaars (*Riding the Waves of Culture*), "Organisations do not simply react to their environment as a ship might to waves. They actively select, interpret, choose and create their environments." CEOs don't simply *act on* employees, customers, the community, the market, and the ecology. All are members of a system whose many parts influence and mutually define each other. Likewise, consultants are not just outside experts called upon to diagnose and cure the ills of a company. Any attempt at such allegedly objective observation will of necessity bias both what they see and the results they get. Students of organizational behavior have noted this about the questionnaires management and consultants ask employees of companies to answer. The questions themselves elicit one kind of response. Different questions produce quite different answers, and thus a quite different picture of employee interests, concerns, and attitudes. This is a participatory universe. There is no "out there."

Neither, we know from all the new sciences of this century, is there any basis for the many dualisms of Western tradition. We know now there is no radical split between mind and body. Our state of awareness and ability to think is affected by the health of the body; the health of the body is affected by our psychological state. Our character is affected by our genetic code, but also by the biological and social environment in which those genes flourish. Consciousness behaves differently from matter, but both are patterns of energy on an underlying reality. I firmly believe there is no more basis for a sharp distinction between public and private, between the selves we bring to work and the selves we share with our families and friends. This distinction is an illusion created by mechanistic structures and attitudes, and dissolves with their dissolution.

At Motorola I spoke with a secretary who had worked for years on the shop floor of the components division. This division is run mechanistically. Her boss played by the old rules. "If one of my children got sick," she said, "my boss didn't want to know. I had certain hours I had to be in and a job I had to do, and he didn't care what was going on at home. I hated him and I hated the job and I did just what I was required to do and no more." Now this woman works as a secretary at Motorola University, the training side of the corporation. "My new boss is completely different. He always smiles in the morning and asks how I am. He asks after the husband and the kids. When one of the kids is sick, he tells me not to come in to work. I adore him and I'd do anything for him." Now she puts in extra hours, does things outside her job description, and has volunteered for a training course to become a conference organizer. She works with her whole person, and both she and the job are growing.

In his Scientific Management theory, Frederick Taylor described employees as "passive units of production." But in this participatory universe, no one can be passive. Every action that we take, every attitude that we harbor, every thought that we think reverberates throughout the universe's many interconnections. The least of an organization's employees has the potentiality to be a responsible agent, and thus to bring creativity to the job. Many are now being required to do so. At Shell Oil, a member of the Leadership Council commented, "It used to be that you knew you would have a job for life and eventually settle at the right level of seniority. All you had to do was what you were told. But that's no longer enough. Today, every one of us has to reinvent the job as we go along." That kind of challenge goes beyond doing a job with efficiency. It requires an engagement with meaning.

Vacuum versus Quantum Vacuum

In old paradigm science, the universe is a still, cold, and silent place. Black emptiness fills the space between visible objects. Newtonian scientists are preoccupied with the objects, with their observation, manipulation, and control. They think that objects are all that is. Newtonian organizations and Newtonian leaders concentrate on *doing,* on setting goals and achieving results, on technique.

New paradigm science sees that the universe is a vast pool of seething potentiality, an interwoven pattern of dynamic energies. There is no emptiness. Objects are just surface manifestations of a deeper, underlying source. Quantum or complexity scientists are preoccupied with hidden patterns, with unseen connections, with synchronicity and evolution. They are filled with the adventure and excitement of *becoming.* New paradigm organizations are rooted in their vision. Their leaders focus on *being* as well as doing.

Quantum science tells us, as I have mentioned, that everything in the universe is energy. *Things,* objects on which we can focus—rocks, trees, stars, buildings, animals, ourselves—are all specific, recognizable patterns of dynamic energy. The matter of which these things consist comes and goes, like the water molecules that flow through the funnel of a whirlpool, but the patterns persist. In human beings, the matter that composes our bodies, the molecules of water and fat and protein, changes entirely within every seven-year period. The neural connections in our brains alter every second. And yet we remain recognizable over the years as the individuals that we are. Our overall patterns change only slightly.

Organizations, too, are persisting patterns of dynamic energy. That is why they have character, personality, a recognizable style over the years even though their employees and even their CEOs come and go. At the beginning of this book, I quoted a letter from Andrew Stone in which he described the sixty thousand employees of Marks & Spencer as the individual particles in the company's brain. In other conversations with me, he has spoken of the company's ongoing personality, of its instinct over the years for choosing leaders with different styles or visions because they are the leaders needed at that moment. The company itself, its persisting pattern, is larger than and somehow functions above and beyond the actions and conscious decisions of all its individual parts—the CEOs, the board chairmen, the employees, the shareholders, and so on.

In physics, when we recognize that every existing thing is a pattern of dynamic energy, the question arises: What are these patterns of energy patterns *on?* On what is the universe *written?* The answer is the quantum vacuum. As described by the new physics, the whole universe consists of energy, and the ground state of that energy, the still, unexcited state of source energy, is the quantum vacuum. An Eastern philosopher might describe it as "the Infinite that is the background for the whole." Here in the West it is more difficult to understand the true nature of the quantum vacuum because we take "vacuum" to mean empty. But the quantum vacuum is only empty of *things* and *qualities.* We cannot see it or touch it or measure it, but it is not empty in itself. On the contrary, the quantum vacuum is full with all the potentiality latent in the universe. The concept of such "full emptiness" is common to Eastern thought. As the poet in the Indian *Isha Upanishat* describes it:

There is an endless world, O my brother

And there is a nameless Being of whom nought can be said.

Only he knows who has reached that region:

It is other than all that is heard and said.

No form, no body, no length, no breadth, is seen there:

How can I tell you that which it is?

Kabir says: It cannot be told by the words of the mouth,

It cannot be written on paper:

It is like a dumb person who tastes a sweet thing—how shall it be explained?

The quantum vacuum, then, is an equivalent from twentieth-century physics of the Hindu Brahma. It is a concept similar to the Buddhist *Sunyata,* the Void. It is what the Western psychologist Carl Jung would call the Self that is the source of self. In physics, it is the ground state and source of our world and of human existence. Existing things—ourselves, our thoughts, our decisions, rocks and trees and all physical things both living and nonliving—are "excitations," or waves, on the still pond of the quantum vacuum. To *"ex-ist"* in the original Latin literally means "to stand out from," and that is what existing things do. They stand out from the quantum vacuum. That still pond of energy provides the ultimate vision for the universe's unfolding. It is the source of all vision and value as we know them.

In the most literal sense, human organizations are self-organizing systems written on the quantum vacuum. They, too, are "ex-isting" things. And just as each individual existing thing is one finite or limited expression of the infinite potentiality of the universe as a whole, so each human organization is rooted in and is a finite expression of that pool of vision that nourishes the whole of creation. The vision of an organization drives the organization. It is expressed in its style of leadership, in its style of doing business, in the basic values that inspire its spoken and unspoken code of practice.

At Marks & Spencer, which began as a small, family-owned business, those values are still rooted in the basic values of the Jewish spiritual tradition. Judaism is a religion that celebrates the sanctity of community life. For a good Jew, it is a holy duty to supply the needs of the community. A butcher, a baker, or a haberdasher is a holy man just as much as a rabbi. Today's very modern and very secular and frequently non-Jewish directors of the M&S global concern still speak privately among themselves of satisfying their customers' wish to feel happy about themselves, of turning out products that put smiles on people's faces. In their 1981 book *The Art of Japanese Management*, Richard Pascle and Anthony Athos point out that Japanese firms like Matsushita Electric list as core company values things like fairness, harmony and cooperation, courtesy and humility, and gratitude. These, of course, are core spiritual values of the Buddhist tradition.

Newtonian organizations seek their identity in technique, products, and structure. Their core values are profit, efficiency, success, perhaps excellence (in the service of profit). They seek customer loyalty, and where necessary, customer "satisfaction." They are, to return to the words of James Carse, playing a "finite game," a game played for the purpose of winning. New paradigm organizations (and some of these are very old, very established firms) draw their focus, their energy from a deeper pool of vision and more lasting values. They see themselves as part of some larger tradition. Organizations like Marks & Spencer and Matsushita don't shun profit, success, efficiency, and so on. But these mechanistic values are realized as by-products of deeper spiritual values like service to the community, care for the environment, concern for human happiness.

These companies are playing what Carse calls an "infinite game," a game played for the sake of continuing play. They are concerned with sustainability, their own and that of the communities and environments in which they operate.

4

At the Edge

However it may storm and rage
I thank it,
Because it is cold, and cruel, and ruthless
And yet gives peace.
Become as free as the sea,
Surrender utterly to the sea,
Surrender to uncertainty as the only certainty.

—Par Lagerkvist

The turbulence of the sea, the sometimes tempestuous unpredictability of the weather, the precarious balance of the planets in the solar system, the whirlpools that form in streams and rivers, the ebb and flow of blood through our bodies, and the beating of the human heart. These are all examples of chaotic systems poised at the edge. They are balanced between stability and instability, between predictability and unpredictability. They possess structure and yet at every moment may transmute that internally into new structure. They do work and serve a purpose, but they are not fixed on any goal or locked into any set rhythm and thus are always open to adapting to change. They are sometimes called "open dynamic systems," "self-organizing systems," or "dissipative systems."

At the Volvo Car Corporation in Sweden, people have redesigned the car development process. The old engineering groups were tightly structured, intricately planned, and centrally controlled. Each group member represented a specific function and participated strictly in that role, giving the entire group a regular and determinate pattern. The groups were organized hierarchically to deliver the desired products. Two years ago the company started from scratch with a new idea. Engineers worked together on loosely organized, collective teams and other professionals were brought in as well. Subteams worked within larger teams. Individual engineers were encouraged to move around from one team to another or from one subteam to another within a team. Not just the chairs, but even the desks of the engineers were put on wheels. Says Anne Nihlsson Ehle, Volvo's vice president in charge of change management, "We didn't know what we were going to get out of each team until we had the team. Their way of working together surprised us and them. But it works!" Nihlsson Ehle was inspired by quantum physics. She takes pride in boasting that Volvo is a corporation poised "to think at the edge." Both corporate creativity and productivity have increased, and with them corporate profitability.

> At Volvo, even the desks are put on wheels.

At Marks & Spencer, Andrew Stone discourages his managers from coming to divisional meetings with formal reports. "Just come with your ideas and your enthusiasm, and let's see what happens." As we have seen, a spirit of play predominates at these meetings. And yet serious things get done. Decisions are taken and product lines emerge. The retail market is chaotic, driven by the whim of fashion, economic fluctuation, uncertain competition, social and political instability, changes in the buying power of different age groups, demographic shifts, cross-cultural influences, links between taste and wider cultural shifts. For over a hundred years Marks & Spencer has thrived at the edge of this chaos. The company has a genius for choosing leaders and leadership styles that are right for the moment.

In chaos theory, *the edge* is not a precipice. It is not something we can fall off, like the edge of a table or the edge of a cliff. Being "at the edge" is not the same as being "on the edge," or "over the edge." Being at the edge is a risky and exciting place to be, but in a different sense. In chaos theory, the edge is the border between order and chaos, the point at which self-organization arises from the meeting of stability and instability.

We have all seen natural systems poised at the edge, but may not have been aware of the dynamics unfolding before our eyes. Take the simple case of standing on a bridge watching the flow of a river or a stream. Upstream, the water is smooth, flowing evenly without perturbation, scarcely a ripple on its glassy surface. Then, just beneath us, the water encounters some twigs or rocks. At this point its surface parts and the water forms itself into a series of whirlpools. The whirlpools dance around the obstructions, constantly changing their sizes and their shapes but always maintaining a distinctive, coherent pattern. Then, just beyond the whirlpools, the water fragments completely into white turbulence.

Where the water upstream is smooth, it is in a state of order. And its structure contains information. In nature and in computing systems, information is nothing but structure we can access. An ordered structure contains a certain set amount of information. A simple structure contains less information than a complex one. There is, for instance, more information in a human fingerprint than in a simple drawing containing only a few lines, more information in the hologram of a jungle scene than in a black-and-white photo of the same. But however simple or complex the structure, if it is ordered, the information that it contains is fixed. Reliable, accessible, but ultimately limited. Order means reliability, predictability, and control. But it also means limitation.

The chaotic state of the water, where it has fragmented into white turbulence, may contain information, but if so it is useless to us. Its structure is either so complex or simply so nonexistent that we can't access it. Information *is* nonrandomness. A system that is totally chaotic is a system totally out of control.

At the point where the river meets the stones or the twigs and forms itself into whirlpools, it is poised delicately between order and chaos, between being in control and out of control. This is the point at which its water molecules self-organize into a new, coherent pattern. A whirlpool is nature's most simple example of a self-organizing, open dynamic system. Such systems create *new* order, manufacture *new* information. They are neither in control nor out of control but poised delicately between the two, adaptive and creative. The river's whirlpools change their size and shape. Their inner pattern evolves in dialogue with their environment, as they wrap themselves around the stones or twigs, but it remains recognizable as the pattern of a whirlpool.

We are surrounded by such self-organizing systems. We *are* such self-organizing systems! Each of us is, essentially, a self-organizing pattern of dynamic energy. Indeed, according to the most advanced physics, quantum field theory, everything that exists is a whirlpool in the quantum vacuum—the ground energy state of the universe. The solidity that we take for granted about ourselves, the resistance that we feel when we thump our arms or legs with our supposedly solid hands, is just a transient phenomenon, an illusion of corporeal identity. As I said earlier, seven years ago, not one single molecule of which my body is made today was any part of me. Molecules come and go from my system at every second. The air molecules that I breath in are breathed out within seconds. Most of the water molecules that I drink are passed out within hours, the food molecules within a day or two. Some of these substances that I take in become muscle, fat or protein molecules, brain cells, and these remain part of me somewhat longer. But within a seven-year cycle, every molecule has been exchanged.

What persists about me during and beyond those seven years is a self-organizing pattern. It is that pattern that my distant relatives recognize when they see me after an absence of several years, not the molecules circulating within it. And, like the shifting boundaries of the whirlpools dancing around the obstructing rocks, my own pattern changes and evolves over the years. I both am and am not the five-year-old child my great-aunt from Toledo once held on her knee. I both do and do not resemble my teenage photograph, my wedding photos, and so on. The same is true of corporations and other human organizations. They are patterns that have persisted over the years. The successful ones are patterns that have evolved.

All biological systems, from the simplest bacterium to things as complicated as ourselves and our organizations, are self-organizing patterns of dynamic energy poised at the edge of chaos. This is the secret of life's ability to creatively adapt to changing conditions. And it gives the lie to the previous, old paradigm belief that all balanced systems tend toward stability.

The Fallacy of Stability

Even the most forward-looking companies find themselves trapped in a belief in the importance, and if not the inevitability, then the desireability of stability. This is one Newtonian assumption that dies hard. In economics, in politics, and in business we still live with the paradigm of law-abiding, separate working parts that will, if left to themselves, reach a state of equilibrium. This is the guiding assumption of laissez-faire capitalism, inspired by the Newtonian economics of Adam Smith. And if the system doesn't stabilize itself, then checks and balances meant to dampen down any positive feedback should be built in—like the cybernetic control of a central heating system whose thermostat kicks on or off as necessary to keep the room temperature stable.

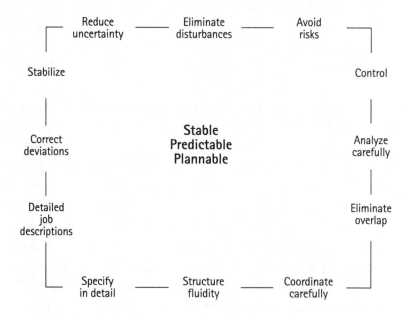

Figure 6. Business as Usual
Source: © 1990, The Foresight Group. Adapted for use with permission.

At a global communications company based in the United States, one of the architects of the new leadership renewal program spoke to me for over an hour about the new physics, chaos and quantum theory, and the important lessons these hold out for companies. Yet when he showed me the new course plan for leadership development, its central focus turned out to be the crucial importance of stability. "All systems tend towards stability," blared out from the page. The new leadership program, among other things, has been designed to enshrine this value. This is what my colleagues at the Foresight Group in Sweden call the "Business as Usual" paradigm (Figure 6).

"Business as usual" in this very mechanistic way of looking at things, whether the business of business or the business of Newtonian science, is about reducing uncertainty and eliminating disturbances, and therefore about avoiding risks and structuring any fluidity. It is about dampening down positive feedback, influences from within or without that might rock the boat.

When I queried his juxtaposition of the new science with a goal of reaching stability, the global communications executive used the example of the human immune system, how it supposedly stabilizes itself to fight off disease. But this is precisely what the immune system does *not* do. The alien viruses and bacteria that invade our bodies mutate constantly, always trying to evade the immune system's defenses. The only way the immune system can stay one step ahead of its enemies is to be poised at the edge of *instability*, ready to evolve in any direction required at a moment's notice. Instability underpins the immune system's flexibility, its adaptability. It is the same with most of our biological functions, including creative thought and much of our learning ability.

California biologist Walter Freeman has done pioneering research on the role played by chaos in our sense of smell. Freeman's work was actually conducted on the olfactory system of rabbits, but the structures of the olfactory system are highly conservative and remarkably consistent across the whole range of mammalian life. The nerve endings in the olfactory bulb, the brain's center of smell, are delicately poised between stability and instability. When we sense a familiar smell, one that the olfactory bulb has already wired into its recognition system, the firings of the various nerve endings involved quickly settle into an ordered state. Existing wiring can deal with existing information. But when the olfactory nerve endings are exposed to no odor, or to an unfamiliar odor, the nerve endings fire irregularly across all possible frequencies and amplitudes, poised to respond quickly to any change in input. This chaotic state allows the olfactory bulb to rewire itself to deal with new information.

Similar research has been done exposing the role of chaotic instability in human visual processing, and this has led brain scientists to
speculate that chaos plays a crucial role in many human learning
processes, as well as in concentration and decision making. It is precisely
because the nerve endings at our neural junctions (synapses) can fire
wildly across large spectra of frequencies and amplitudes, feeling their way
toward the most stable patterns, that the brain can wire and rewire itself
in dialogue with experience.

So the infant's brain is poised at the edge. Chaotic instability in its
initial neural firings enables the brain to adapt to the physical and cultural conditions in which it finds itself. It is this chaos that allows the brain
to be nature's most effective "learning organization," and children its most
effective practitioners.

Children are such successful open dynamic systems, such effective
learning organizations, precisely because they are not yet wired up. We
have seen that in our culture, it takes roughly eighteen years for young
people to lay down sufficient neural connections to deal with the usual
challenges they face. During that time, each child's growing mind is
poised at the edge, driven by curiosity and using play, imagination, and
mistakes to learn and to wire itself according to necessity. During this
period of growth, the young brain uses huge amounts of energy and
requires a compensatory amount of rest and sleep.

Young corporations wire their growing corporate brains in much the
same way, combining a rich mix of vision, experimentation (play!), imagination, curiosity, chaos, mistakes, and learning in laying down the style,
habits, and infrastructures of the expanding company. These young corporate brains are flexible, sometimes a little unsteady. They make mistakes,
and the ones that succeed learn from them. There is a great deal of litera-
ture on the role "creative mistakes" have played in the developing careers
of some of industry's leading entrepreneurs. For instance, as John Micklethwait and Adrian Wooldridge observe in their 1996 book *The Witch
Doctors*, "[Jack] Welch was first noticed at General Electric in the 1960s
because he ran a plastics plant that blew up. As a young entrepreneur,
Richard Branson spent a night in a police cell after smuggling records into
Britain from France. Rupert Murdoch nearly went bust on several occasions at the beginning of the 1990s. Babe Ruth may have been best known

for his home runs, but he also set a record for strike-outs." It is well-known that the Hungarian financier George Soros, who has made billions by playing the uncertainties of the stock market, has also lost billions.

Soros has named his main investment fund "The Quantum Fund." He has done so, he says, because of the insight Heisenberg's Uncertainty Principle has given him into the inherent instability of free markets and open societies—societies that allow free expression, dissent, and a recognition that many points of view should flower because all points of view are somewhat flawed. In Newtonian science, there is an assumption that the observer and the observed are independent. A Newtonian physicist can measure a system with any instrument from any vantage point in absolute space-time and always get the same result. Reality is "out there." Adam Smith's Newtonian laissez-faire economics assumed the same about markets and customers, about prices, supply, and demand.

In consequence, Soros points out in the January 1997 *Atlantic Monthly,* classic economic theory "has managed to create an artificial world in which the participants' preferences and the opportunities confronting participants are independent of each other, and prices tend towards an equilibrium that brings the two forces into balance."

But quantum mechanics and a more honest appraisal of human behavior show us otherwise. According to Heisenberg's Uncertainty Principle, the observer and the observed are inextricably linked. If a quantum scientist asks a particle question, a particle answer emerges from the experiment. As noted in Chapter Three, a wave question results in a wave answer. Soros extends this to economic activity, where he sees prices and preferences, values and preferences, preferences and demand as inextricably linked, and the whole mix as poised on the brink of instability.

"In financial markets," he argues, "prices are not merely the passive reflection of independently given demand and supply; they also play an active role in shaping those preferences and opportunities. This reflexive interaction renders financial markets inherently unstable." If, for instance, most investors think a stock will be attractive to other investors, the price of the stock will jump. This is an instance of "positive feedback" leading to instability.

Open, truly democratic societies and wholly laissez-faire markets are poised on the brink of instability. Hence their creativity but also the necessity for some centrally imposed checks and balances and the temptation of totalitarian regimes to impose total central control. Total freedom, lack of all checks and balances, risks chaos. Total control in a quest for imposed and therefore reliable equilibrium costs freedom and inevitably results in a system that runs down from a lack of its own internal, creative instability—as "closed systems" do in nature. Nature works with an uncertain system of positive and negative feedbacks, and the negative feedbacks don't always keep the positive ones in check. It is massive, chaotic fluctuations that push evolution forward. This is the paradox of "leadership at the edge," and there is no set formula (as in Newtonian physics!) for getting the balance right.

We face the same paradox in our creative thinking processes and the design of our corporate infrastructures. A learning, creative brain uses more energy than the whole rest of the body put together. Out of the box, at-the-edge thinking uses as much energy as a game of rugby football. If we were creative all the time, we would get exhausted. So our brains are designed to conserve energy as well as use it. The whole point of wiring up all those neural connections in childhood is so that we can use them later reliably and at least semiautomatically. Habit can be a wonderful thing! Reliable corporate infrastructures, hierarchies, habits, and chains of command can make leadership a lot less stressful. Second- and third-generation corporate leadership can (or at least *used* to be able to) do a good job sailing the ship with sound managerial skills.

By about the age of eighteen, it used to be possible for most—it is still possible for some—adult brains to slow down. But going onto automatic pilot, relying on the learning and lessons of the past, relying on training, habit, and precedent—on competence—only works if the environment in which we have to function is the same environment in which we wired up our brains. For a vast number of adults today, for most corporate leaders, such environmental stability is itself a thing of the past.

A Whole Culture at the Edge

In his recent and devastatingly powerful account of life in the twentieth century, *The Age of Extremes,* British historian Eric Hobsbawm points out that there has been more change in the past fifty years, globally, than since the Stone Age. Transportation and communication, of course, have been revolutionized, and with them social and economic expectations and possibilities. When I was an undergraduate at MIT in the early 1960s, we had one mainframe computer on campus, and it occupied a huge room. Only the most science-fiction-minded of our professors envisaged the desktop PC and its information revolution. Top executives at IBM certainly didn't! Only a handful of today's top executives are comfortable with this revolution and most billion-dollar-company Information Technology systems are underemployed or not fully applied. They have been slotted in, as an afterthought, to company infrastructures designed to block, or at best not to use, the free flow of instantaneous information.

But not just travel and communication have changed beyond recognition in this past half-century. We are heading into the new millennium with our social, religious, and family institutions all up for reinvention. Both domestic crime rates and corporate and political scandals expose the fragility of our moral code, the general lack of moral conviction, moral common sense, and leadership. Technological breakthroughs like genetic engineering have outpaced our ability to use them wisely.

Along with his remarks on the inherent instability of laissez-faire market economies, George Soros mentions this crisis of values and its own contribution to general cultural instability. Adam Smith and his contemporaries could take stable societal values as a given, and could rightly assume that a set of moral principles outside the market mechanism would help to keep that mechanism itself at some equilibrium. This is no longer true. Now, says Soros:

> As the market mechanism has extended its sway, the fiction that people act on the basis of a given set of non-market values has become progressively more difficult to maintain. Advertising, marketing, even packaging, aim at shaping people's preferences rather than merely responding to them. . . . Unsure of what they stand for, people increasingly rely on money as the criterion of value. What is more expensive is considered better. What used to be the medium of exchange has usurped the place of fundamental values. . . . The cult of success has replaced a belief in principles. Society has lost its anchor.

At the same time, and on another level, the identity and identity-conferring power of the nation-state have greatly diminished. Globalization has destroyed the meaning and usefulness of national boundaries so rapidly that politicians cannot keep pace. A new global culture rich in universal values has yet to emerge. Space and time themselves must find some new meaning.

It has been exactly a hundred years since Nietzsche announced the death of God, and finally, today, we are face to face with that reality. Nietzsche didn't mean specifically the death of religion, but rather the death of our whole cultural framework, the end of our paradigm. It is terrifying, but it is also filled with infinite opportunity. The death of one paradigm usually heralds the birth of another, and those who inherit the new one often wonder what all the fuss was about. But ours is a generation at the edge, a generation poised (or torn!) between the old, dying paradigm and the ambiguous outlines of the new one waiting to be born. The neural connections we grew in childhood won't carry us through our turbulent adult years. Ours is a generation that must wire and rewire our brains, that must invent new categories, new concepts, new patterns, new organizational structures, new leadership. Those of us with children experience this daily in the difficulty of making up the rules as we go along. As Nietzsche pointed out, we can no longer get by just following given values. We have to create new ones.

Those leading companies find their jobs demanding in a way never experienced before by second- and third- and fourth-generation managers. Managing an existing system is no longer enough when no system can afford to be stable. Leadership at the edge requires all the poise, the gut instinct, the risk taking, the wide-ranging imagination, and the creative mistakes of the child, the artist, or the founding entrepreneur.

The book in which Nietzsche announced the death of God was called *Thus Spoke Zarathustra*. The book opens with the people of a village gathering in the village square to watch a tightrope walker perform his act. According to the story, the tightrope walker must walk a rope stretched between the Towers of Certainty. He doesn't make it. In the book, the tightrope walker falls off and is killed. Nietzsche shakes his head with sadness and says, "He wasn't ready yet." Now, a century later, that is the trick every one of us is called upon to perform.

In some of the training seminars I run with a partner, we offer people on the course something called "the concept cafe." This is an evening dinner at which each of the participants is asked to read some famous quote and reflect on its implications for their personal and working lives. One of the quotes we often use is by the Irish poet Arthur William Edgar O'Shaughnessy, a poem called "The Music Makers." O'Shaughnessy's poem was written to describe the creative role of poets and other artists, people who in any culture live and work at the edge. Today it seems to apply to most of us.

> We are the music makers,
>> And we are the dreamers of dreams. . . .
> Yet we are the movers and shakers
>> Of the world forever it seems.
> We, in the ages lying,
>> In the buried past of the earth,
> Built Nineveh with our sighing,
>> And Babel itself with our mirth;
> And o'erthrew them with prophesying
>> To the old of the new world's worth;
> For each age is a dream that is dying,
>> Or one that is coming to birth.

At the Edge of the Management/Leadership Paradigms

Much of this book is about paradigms and their impact on business thinking and corporate infrastructures. O'Shaughnessy's poem is about the death of an old paradigm and the birth of a new. In earlier pages I have focused on surfacing the extent to which business and management theory are in the grip of Newtonian thinking, and how we might shift that to a new perspective offered by quantum thinking. Taken at this simple level, I seem to be offering readers my own Towers of Certainty, and the task of moving from one to the other. I have something much more difficult in mind, but let's focus for a moment on the two towers, the choice between Newtonian management and quantum leadership. What would it look like in detail?

The Newtonian paradigm, we saw earlier, describes a world that is simple and law-abiding. It is a world framed in certainty, a world we can control. The quantum paradigm, by contrast, describes a world that is complex and chaotic, a world that is uncertain. Any attempt to dissect the complexity or to regulate the uncertainty with hands-on control reins in, or even destroys, everything that is rich, interesting, and creative about a natural self-organizing system.

In Table 1, I have constructed a chart that puts the features of these two contrasting paradigms in management and leadership terms. The left-hand column takes the features most prominent in Newtonian physics and sums them up as a management theory. This is very familiar territory. It is straightforward Taylorian Scientific Management that we can find in any MBA textbook.

Taylorian management stresses the values of certainty and predictability. This is a corporate world governed by inner laws and hands-on control, a world where blueprints and five-year plans are inviolate. This is goal-oriented, results-oriented "management by objectives." It is a world of hierarchy, where power emanates from the top or from the center. (This can be quite explicit, as in the plant manager's statement quoted earlier: "It is the business of management to manage and of unions to react.") Just as Newtonian physics sees the atoms as passive units of matter operated upon by universal forces, Taylorian management sees workers as passive units of production, subject to the goals and control of management. Employees are company resources—"human resources"—like coal or iron or silicon chips. Employees are most easily controlled, and give their maximum productive output, if divided into separate labor functions. Remember Adam Smith's pin factory. Lines of command and rules of control are inflexible. Organization is rule-bound, heavily bureaucratic. Where Newton argued that there is one absolute perspective on space-time, a God's eye view of the universe, Taylor argued that there is a single point of view in management thinking, one best way for any company to proceed. We can discuss and we can brainstorm, but the ultimate point is to find the one best way forward. Where Darwinian biology extended Newtonian thinking to the importance of competition between species, to survival of the fittest, Taylor stressed the inevitability and the benefit of competition between companies and within divisions of the same company. Competition keeps us on our toes. It weeds out the weak.

Newtonian Management Stresses	Quantum Management Stresses
Certainty	Uncertainty
Predictability	Rapid change; unpredictability
Hierarchy	Nonhierarchical networks
Division of labor or function fragmentation	Multifunctional and holistic (integrated) effort
Power emanates from top or center	Power emanates from many interacting centers
Employees are passive units of production	Employees are cocreative partners
Single viewpoint; one best way	Many viewpoints; many ways of getting things done
Competition	Cooperation
Inflexible structures; heavy on bureaucratic control	Responsive and flexible structures; hands-off supervision
Efficiency	Meaningful service and relationships
Top-down (reactive) operation	Bottom-up (experimental) operation

Table 1. Management-Leadership Chart

Like Newton's machines, the prime value of Taylorian companies is efficiency, the most output for the least input. Even in very recent years, this led to the ultimate Taylorian practices of downsizing and reengineering. And finally, like those billiard balls in the void, Taylorian companies are "reactive." They bounce off changes in the environment, in the market, in the competition. They *react* to changes, they don't initiate change.

The right-hand column of Table 1 is very different. It is also less familiar and more open to question and further suggestion because I made it up myself. I have constructed a chart of quantum leadership emphases by trying to do a Taylor with quantum concepts. I have consciously matched key quantum physical ideas to aspects of leadership in an attempt to outline the key points of a new leadership paradigm. This right-hand column has emerged from my work and conversation with companies over the past several years. Most of the quantum characteristics are things I have noticed companies needing, qualities they might benefit from developing, or qualities that leaders themselves within companies have been struggling to articulate. A few of the qualities in this right-hand column are very familiar because they have become buzzwords of the "new management," though many of the company people with whom I work feel these buzzwords are more often talked about than implemented or deeply thought through.

With its Uncertainty Principle and indeterminism, a quantum paradigm in leadership would certainly emphasize uncertainty instead of certainty. It would see uncertainty not as a pitfall but as an opportunity. "We need some uncertainty here to give us room to think," as the Marks & Spencer manager said. Similarly, quantum leadership would take on board the rapid changes and unpredictability that confront business today but would see these not so much as, or not just as, a problem but as an opportunity. Quantum organizations would not just learn to tolerate or to survive rapid change and unpredictability. They would learn to thrive on them. To do this, they would be less concerned with hierarchy, develop many interacting centers of power and decision making, and create more responsive and flexible, more hands-off infrastructures within the organization. Those Volvo car-making teams are an example of this. So are some of the most prominent features of the Visa credit card company, which I shall discuss in Chapter Six.

Quantum physics recognizes that we live in a participative universe in which living beings are cocreative insiders. We help to make reality happen. The observer is always *inside*, always *a part of*, the observed reality. None of us can avoid our active role in the makeup of things. "The buck stops here." In a quantum organization, employees are not passive units of production. They are not even "intellectual capital," to be invested as

88

the company feels wise. Employees *are* the company. Even the most humble employee has a personality, a way of interacting with fellows, a point of view, a talent that, if unleashed, can help to create the very fabric of the company. Some recognition is given to this with all the talk about "empowerment," but I have encountered some cynicism among those supposedly empowered. Too often they feel it means being asked to shoulder more work or more responsibility for less reward or recognition. Genuine empowerment means redesigning the infrastructures within which people interact with each other and with the company as a whole.

Where Taylor felt certain there was one best path for a company to follow, one best way from A to B, quantum leadership would recognize the value of surfacing and considering many points of view. Quantum systems follow many paths in getting from A to B, and sometimes they arrive at D or E or F instead of B, which may be a pleasant surprise. Quantum leadership is less goal-oriented and more process-oriented. More concerned with what might emerge from putting ideas or processes or teams together than with blueprinting in definite expectations in the original design. It taps into the energy the Volvo manager described: "We didn't know what we were going to get out of each team until we had the team. Their way of working together surprised us and them. But it works!"

Where the Newtonian (Taylorian) company divides itself into competing divisions and divides the market into competing companies, the quantum organization, inspired by the holistic, interacting, cocreative nature of the physical universe, sees the gain to be had from cooperation. Divide C into A and B, and all we have is A and B. Put A and B together in a cooperative, holistic unit and we get a C that is larger than the sum of its parts. As I earlier quoted a Motorola executive saying, "At Motorola we have learned that our competitors are also our suppliers and our customers." Competition is a win-lose situation. Cooperation can be win-win.

Increasingly in management circles there is much talk about meaning and service, about value-driven companies. Too often things like TQM, valuable in themselves, are taken on by Western companies for the real motive of increasing efficiency. Reliable service can be interpreted as yet another competitive device, a way to earn the loyalty of the market.

And values can be mistaken for those things that appear in vision statements. Quantum physics, with its contextualism and observer participation, necessarily raises questions of meaning and value at a more profound level.

On a quantum view, a company's community, its customers, its environment are as much in the company as the company is in or surrounded by them. (The fish is in the water, but the water is also in the fish.) There can be no hard-and-fast boundary between service to the community or service to one's customers and the community's or the customers' service (loyalty, financial support, employee provision) to the company. When Motorola and Marks & Spencer contribute to local education programs and local education budgets, they serve both the community and their own future employees and customers. When Motorola floods a closed Chinese society with cellular phones, the company cocreates the very (more open) environment in which it will function. It is selling *communication,* not just telephones. Quantum leaders are not just their nine-to-five ability to command and control. They are their whole history, their whole character, their deepest personal visions and values. (See Chapter Nine on servant leadership for more discussion of this point.)

And for similar contextualist and holistic reasons, a quantum organization realizes that it cannot just react to its environment or to events. Top-down control is not just insufficient; it can be damaging. Bottom-up experimentation and flexible infrastructures and reward schemes for risk taking are crucial to a company's own creative adaptation to the changing environment and to its creative cocreation of that environment.

Not Either-Or but Both-And

Quantum physics has not superseded Newtonian physics. It does not make it wrong—or even less valuable. On the contrary, quantum physics contains the truth of Newtonian physics within itself. If we want to build a bridge or put a man on the moon, it is still Newtonian equations we will use to do our calculations. It is just that, given the newer quantum perspective, we now know that Newtonian physics is valid only over a certain narrow range of experience. For larger systems, we need relativity theory; for smaller ones, quantum theory. One day, undoubtedly, there will be a further physics that will incorporate quantum physics and relativity theory within its own still larger perspective. There is no limit to the recontextualizing vision of expanding science.

By the same token, there is nothing wrong with the left-hand column of Table 1. There are times when it is appropriate to be certain, to have definite goals, to control situations, to provide structure, and to do all the other things called for by Taylorian management theory. It is a useful management approach for much that same part of experience handled by left-brain activity, the brain's logical, analytical hemisphere. But the brain has a right hemisphere, too, that is more intuitive, and like the right-hand column of Table 1, it comes into its own in quite different situations. There are situations in which it is better to let the imagination run, not to pin ourselves down or limit ourselves to definite goals, not to control or constrain things too tightly. Any company that wants to stay in business has to worry about its bottom line (efficiency), but a sole concern with that can limit growth, expansion, risk taking, experiment, and vision.

We have seen that our brain works so creatively because our serial and parallel thought processes are integrated by a third kind of thinking that is poised between order and chaos. The brain is also designed to use both its left and right hemispheres in unison, and these are joined at the corpus callosum. If this dialogue between the two hemispheres is broken, as is sometimes done to treat very bad epilepsy, our field of consciousness splits and each hemisphere is less effective. Similarly, so-called normal, conservative science limits itself to working within a paradigm, but then all it can do is ratify that paradigm. It is revolutionary science, working at the edge of paradigms, that moves knowledge forward. It can see the strengths and limitations of various paradigms, and can create entirely new ones.

My real point in drawing up the Management-Leadership Chart shown in Table 1, then, is not to offer two towers of certainty, one superior to the other. It is more to offer the vision of what "leadership at the edge" would look like, leadership that is aware of different paradigms, leadership that can assess the worth of a given paradigm for a given context and choose between options. And leadership that can invent new paradigms when necessary. Both-and, not either-or.

Marks & Spencer has two very different sorts of leaders at the top of the company, their different styles likened by some observers to Newtonian and quantum. Sir Richard Greenbury, the chairman, is a more orthodox manager, a command-and-control, let's-get-the-job-done sort of leader. As we have seen, Andrew Stone, one of his four joint managing directors, is much more at home with a quantum style of leadership. The two men's leadership styles clash. There is friction between them, yet mutual respect. Outsiders attribute the success of Marks & Spencer to its ability to have both those very different leadership styles working in partnership. Similarly, Andrew Stone has thirteen directors reporting to him, three of whom are on the main board. They often disapprove of his leadership style and of the decisions he makes. Every week Stone invites those three critics to his office for a "bitch session." They shout at each other, they are rude, they surface their grievances—and then they all work together as a team more effectively.

Individuals are not all the same. Some personality types are more at home with uncertainty and ambiguity than others. Some have a higher threshold for chaos than others. Some like to be creative, to think and act out of the box. Others panic if expected to do so. Some, in short, prefer left-column management, others right-column leadership. "Leadership at the edge" also means being able to get the best out of both these types, and to use the strengths of each for the company as a whole. My friend R.S. Moorthy, director of the Culture and Technology Section at Motorola University, has shared the following thought with me.

Moorthy reckons that in any large company, 5 percent, or at very most 10 percent, of employees are heretical, freewheeling, out-of-the-box types. These people need a long lead so as to be creative. They always want to change things and they lead that change. There are another 5 percent in the company who will never change, no matter how they are led. The bulk of the company is that 85 percent (or 90 percent) majority who don't initiate change and aren't comfortable with change if it is too quick, but who will change if properly led and properly motivated. (See Figure 7.) The leader of an innovative company must be poised at the edge between those 5 percent out-of-the-box types and the 85 percent mass. It is essential to be sufficiently open to the needs and the thinking of those who challenge even the leader's thinking, and also the needs and the thinking of those who need to be led. The real success of the company depends upon keeping the contributions of the two populations integrated.

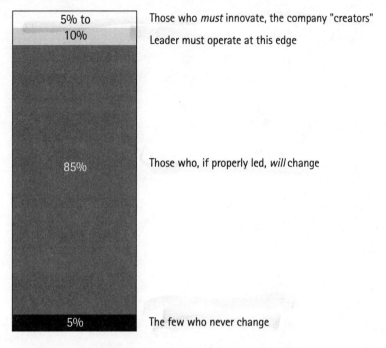

Figure 7.   Willingness to Change: R.S. Moorthy's Model

Such reflection on personality types and thresholds for uncertainty takes us back to the nature of the human self and the different organizational structures derived from differing models of the self. Let us go on now to look at that.

Structure and Leadership of the Rewired Corporation

- Three Kinds of Thinking
- Three Concepts of the Self
- Three Kinds of Organization

In his recent book on the world in the year 2020, British financial writer Hamish McRae forecast that within the next quarter-century such "old motors of growth" as land, capital, and natural resources would become less crucial to national and corporate economic success. Instead, he argued, future success would depend more on "qualitative features" like the quality, organization, motivation, and self-discipline of people. These, in turn, I believe, hinge crucially on our working concept of the human self and our ability to draw out its potentialities.

Our concept of the self includes things like our personal identity and personal boundaries—what is inside or outside of the self? How much of "me" is really me? For how much of myself am I responsible and how much is beyond my control? How much is within the control of my genes, my upbringing, my education, my training? How does one individual self relate to another or to a group or an organization? Do we need to manage or control these relationships—and if so, how? What damages or nourishes the self, and thus what motivates it? From where does the self derive its own sense of self-worth and its wider notions of meaning and value? How do I, as an individual self, assess the worth of another? Do I derive my authority, my ability to act and to choose, from qualities within myself or do I seek authority, wisdom, and discipline from outside myself—from parents, society, religious bodies, or corporate organizations?

Such questions are vital to organizational theory and practice. Organizations organize people—human selves. Organizational theory is based on a culture's answers to questions about the self. The success or failure of organizational practice depends upon how closely these answers fit the reality. If we think people are constituted in a certain way, we will create laws, expectations, and organizational structures accordingly. If people are not in fact like our concept of them, the structures may well fail. At best, inadequate structures will limit or distort the human qualities they had hoped to organize.

It is the central thesis of this book that thinking structures in the human brain are the prototypes of human organizational structures that we evolve or design. There are three kinds of structures in the brain, each responsible for a different kind of thinking. We saw in Chapter Two that serial, one-on-one neural tracts embed our logical, rational, goal-oriented thinking, our problem-solving, how-to thinking. Parallel or neural network structures embed our associative thinking, the emotion-centered, body-centered thinking with which we recognize patterns, learn skills, form habits and emotional associations, and store tacit knowledge, knowledge that we can't communicate through rules and manuals. Neural oscillations, perhaps quantum in origin, integrate our serial and parallel thinking processes and form a third kind of brain structure. These are responsible for our creative, insightful thinking, for our ability to create new concepts and new patterns, to challenge our assumptions and change our mental models, to adapt to rapid change and radically new situations.

Each of these three brain thinking structures also underlies, I believe, a quite distinct model of the human self and its potentialities. These three models of the self lead, in turn, to three different models for human organization and for control and development within organizations. This next section of the book will be devoted to exploring these, their infrastructures, and their leadership.

In neuroscience, we saw, the serial and parallel structures for thinking are well-researched and well-understood. Both have been successfully modeled as types of computing systems. One-on-one neural tracts are the model for serial processing PCs. Parallel neural networks are the model for parallel processors, or neural network computers. Broadly speaking, the two associated models of self and their accompanying models of organization are also familiar. Both have been written about extensively by sociologists and organization theorists, though seldom as coherent models of self and organization, and never in association with underlying brain structures.

One familiar model of self and organization is the dominant Western model. This model describes an individualist self organized in a rule-bound (or law-bound), contractual, and often bureaucratic structure. The other familiar model of self and organization predominates in the East, particularly in Confucian society. This model describes a self that is contextual and relational, defined wholly or largely in terms of associations—

household, extended family, village, work community, and so on. This self is organized in complex and ambiguous networked structures bound by habit, custom, and tradition. The two models have been described succinctly by Chinese sociologist Fei Xiaotong as "the two basic types of society." "One type of society," writes Fei in his 1992 book *From the Soil,* "forms as a natural result of people growing up together, and has no other purpose than being simply an outgrowth of human interaction. The other type of society is that which has been organized explicitly to fulfill goals. . . . The first is an example of organic solidarity and the second an example of mechanical solidarity." I have found this book invaluable. It makes the difference between Eastern and Western societies (and hence organizations) very clear, and was crucial to my own insight that a society's model of the self underpins its theories of organization.

As stated clearly by Fei's use of words, the Western model is mechanistic. It is a Newtonian, atomistic-particle model. Indeed, Fei uses the metaphor of Western individuals seen as isolated straws that can be gathered up into organizational bundles. The Eastern model is wavelike, holistic, every individual ambiguously interwoven with many others. Fei uses the metaphor of Eastern individuals being like stones dropped onto the still surface of a pond, each radiating a pattern outward and the various connecting patterns overlapping and influencing each other. Sociologists usually associate the atomistic Western model with large, anonymous urban societies, and the Eastern model with more close-knit, community-oriented agrarian societies. The whole basis of Fei's Confucian sociology is that the Chinese are essentially a peasant people rooted to the land. Even those who have migrated to large urban areas keep their traditional landed patterns of association.

In organization studies, small new companies still led by the inspirational founder are often compared to networked agrarian societies. Everyone knows everyone else; formal rules are less important than customs, relationships, and associations; new ideas and new products evolve through inspiration, cooperation, trial and error; and the personality and vision of the founder-leader somehow suffuses and guides the whole network. These small-company infrastructures tend to be informal and flexible. But such small companies, if they grow and succeed, usually evolve in the second and third generation into large, anonymous, bureaucratic organizations of the Western type. Something is gained on the level of scale and organization by this transition, but the personal, inspirational, and associative qualities of the small company are usually lost. Infrastructures become more rigid, adaptation to change less easy. A new kind of leadership is demanded.

Inspired by the new science of this century, particularly quantum science, and by the creative thinking structures in the brain, I envisage a further, third model of the self and an accompanying third model of organization. I call these the *quantum self* and the *quantum organization* because of their similarity to quantum physical systems and processes. This third model has the both-and qualities of both particle (individualist) systems and wave (networked) systems—and the further qualities found in the creative thinking and organizational potential of our distinctively human brains.

5

The Western Model:

The Newtonian Self and the Newtonian Organization

While working on this chapter, I spent the day at a North Cornwall seaside pub. The wild gray-and-white surf rolling up on the beach below in gale-force winds was a stark and refreshing distraction from Newtonian ways of looking at the world and its systems. The storm harked back to themes discussed in the last chapter. But taking a break from the view and the current writing, I looked around the pub for something to do inside on a rainy day. There was the customary billiards table tucked away in a corner, its hard, bright-colored balls being manipulated into pockets by men who used an intuitive knowledge of rules and forces to bounce one ball off another in an effort to be the first to clear the table. My mind was brought squarely back to the world of Newtonian objects and their organization.

The billiard ball was Newton's metaphor for the atom, the smallest possible bit of matter. As described in his mechanistic physics, each atom (billiard ball) was isolated in space and time from every other. The atoms bounced about in a void, connected to each other by forces of action and reaction, their movements determined by iron laws of motion that assured universal order and predictability. Each atom was circumscribed by a hard and impenetrable boundary. None could get inside another. When they met, they experienced collision and one or both was knocked off its course. The billiard ball has become a familiar metaphor for the Western self. The game of billiards works just as well as a metaphor for the Western organization.

The Billiard Self

Atomism is much older than Newton's physics, dating back to the ancient Greeks. And the atomistic unit of the self is as old as Christian theology. The Christian soul, too, was portrayed as a discrete entity, a small bundle of holiness placed inside us by God and different from everything else within us or about us. This soul preceded the body and its personal ego and survived both. It was what was essential about us, what mattered, what was worthwhile. And just as Newton's atoms of matter were related to each other and to the larger scheme of things through universal laws of motion, so these atomistic souls were manipulated and controlled by universal forces of Good and Evil, the love of God and His angels, the temptations of the Devil. Souls had no direct relationship to each other. Any interrelation was mediated through universal moral law. Each soul was essentially alone, utterly unique, and in direct relationship only to the Godhead. Salvation or damnation was thus decided according to universal moral principles.

As we saw in Chapter Two, Newtonian atomism influenced modern Western concepts of self and society through Sigmund Freud's scientific psychology and through John Locke's liberal individualism. The Freudian self, like each atom in the void, is tragically isolated, a self to itself but just an object to others. This self is imprisoned within hard boundaries, impinged upon from below (its behavior determined) by the dark forces of instinct and aggression latent in the Id. And it is manipulated from above by the codes and expectations of parents and society, the Superego. There is nothing essentially good about this Freudian self. (Freud was not religious.) The self is just the determined result of its instincts and experiences, and left to itself it is quite selfish and unloving. Society's survival (social control) rests on the expectations of the Superego and on the ability of universal moral and social laws to enforce these.

Even before Newton, the social philosopher Thomas Hobbes formed his view of the self in response to mechanistic notions of the universe. For the Hobbesian self, life was "poor, nasty, brutish, and short" because individuals, the atomistic units of society, were driven by greed and self-interest. Left to themselves, without adequate social control, such individuals would tear each other and society to pieces. No friend of freedom, because freedom meant a lack of control, Hobbes conceived of a firm social contract that would ensure order through strict legislation and enforcement. Following Newton, liberal political philosopher John Locke took a kindlier view of human nature and thus the potentialities of freedom. But Locke, too, felt that the atomistic individual was the basic unit of society and that some form of social control had to legislate the behavior of and relationships among these individuals.

In liberal democracies, following Locke's model, we divide selves into public and private aspects and society itself into a public domain and private life. Through discussion, reflection, legislation, and so on, individuals (or at least majorities) agree upon those things to be shared, and thus controlled by, the public domain and its social contract (constitution, laws, and codes). Everything not included in the proper concern of the public domain is considered private, and individuals should be the sole guardians of their own private lives. Western democracies differ about the scope, size, and power of the public domain, but all agree on the distinction between public and private and the rights of the individual to be protected against too much intrusion.

The sanctity of individual rights emphasizes the burden that Western societies place on privacy and the private self. My real self, the real me that I care about and can reveal when I let my hair down at home, is unique and private. It has boundaries that no one dare invade. Boundaries, indeed, that no one *can* invade, even if I or they wished. "Each of us is alone," wrote the British novelist and intellectual C.P. Snow. "Sometimes we escape from our solitary isolation through brief moments of love or intimacy, but each of us dies alone." This private self is in need of some control, but it should be *self*-control.

My public self, by contrast, includes those aspects of myself I have agreed to share and control over which I have agreed to legislate away. Or perhaps my society has determined that I *have* to legislate them away, but if so, only in so much as all others have done so too. My public self is universalizable, general, the aspects of me that everyone else also possesses, and their control is subject to universal laws and principles that are the same for all members of my society. The boundaries of my public self, too, are sharply defined, and neither my most intimate partner, my neighbor, nor the state must violate them.

Western organizations, like Western societies as a whole, organize and control their members on the basis of firm boundaries and formal rules that are universal for all members of any given category. Any such organization, whether business or social, has criteria for membership. Those who don't meet the criteria are excluded, but just as important, those who are included exclude much of themselves from the organization. Membership in any Western-style organization, even an intimate organization like a nuclear family, requires the member to commit only some part of the self to the organization and its rules. "Nobody can own my soul." "The only organization to which *I* belong is *me*."

Indeed, the identity and stability of typical Western organizations is ensured by excluding the individual, unpredictable, private concerns of members, those things that can't be summarized in general rules. People can belong to the same bridge club for twenty years, and know little more about each other than styles and strategies for playing bridge. Big companies modeled on Newtonian (Taylorian) principles don't want to know the personal problems and family obligations of employees. Local government and health care bureaucracies don't function well with exceptions, with cases that can't be universalized. Most of us find such bureaucracy tedious, and can easily feel alienated within our organizational systems, yet most Western people also find security in the rules and boundaries that divide public life from the private and feel threatened if these are eroded.

Two of the big companies for which I have worked in recent years, a communications company and an oil company, have been involved in transformation programs that attempt to increase personal involvement and personal expression at work, particularly at the managerial level. During one of the communications company workshops, a senior manager commented, "All this talk about being a particular type of person and joining the company 'community.' I feel the company is trying to invade my personal space, trying to take over my identity." At the oil company, another senior manager made a similar comment. "To me, this company has always been a job. Now I feel they are trying to buy my soul." Such comments sharply conflict with others made by managers who feel isolated at work, who suffer because they can't bring "themselves" to work. Indeed, the same conflicting comments might have been uttered at different times by the *same* managers. This is the tragic paradox of the Western self—isolated by choice and yet alienated by that isolation. Lonely, yet unwilling to commit to those more full-fledged intimacies that would defeat loneliness.

This same paradox lies at the heart of corporate debates about loyalty. Employees want a more loyal commitment from their companies to job conditions and security, but they don't want to give all of themselves to the company. Corporations want a greater loyalty from their employees, but they don't want to concern themselves with the "personal problems" of those employees. One of the big corporations for which I have worked has made greater employee loyalty a central theme of its transformation process. "We put a lot of time and money into training people. We expect some loyalty in return." In the next breath, the CEO of this same corporation said, "Don't look to us for lifetime employment. It's a rough world out there and you're on your own."

Newtonian physics grew out of this Western split between soul and body or mind and body, between the public and private spheres of the universe. Newton concentrated on bodies, the physical properties of the universe that all material things have in common, that is, the "public sphere." As a scientist, he had no concern with souls, the "private sphere." The Newtonian ideal was the machine, the clockwork universe that relies solely on its formal rules (the laws of motion) to operate. Following Newton, the machine—seeing human beings and human organizations as machines or parts of machines—became the wider cultural norm.

The Newtonian machine consists of separate and replaceable working parts, each of which is included because it serves a function. The machine itself has been built according to blueprint to serve a function. A good machine is one that works efficiently, each part working in harmony with the others to achieve the desired result, but this never happens organically. The separate parts of a machine work in harmony because they are subject to control. If the machine is a sophisticated cybernetic device like a central heating system, such control is programmed into the machine through an internal system like a thermostat. The great universal clockwork machine is controlled by universal laws of motion. Simpler machines are controlled externally through a human controller.

Billiards and Organization

Frederick Taylor's Scientific Management theory looked to the Newtonian physical model. Both Taylor's vision of the organization and his notions about the role of human beings within an organization were mechanistic. Newtonian business corporations are machines that were designed to make profit through the sale of some product. Their separate employees and separate divisions are organized and controlled according to impersonal (public sphere) rules, by the constraints of a contract—and rules and contracts are designed with efficiency in mind. Those things not having to do with the employee's function are outside the job description, and thus outside both the company's concern and the employee's company responsibility. The boundaries are rigid. The ideal employee in the ideal bureaucracy is replaceable, having a skill that has a market elsewhere or that the company can replace as need be. Such employees work most efficiently when given machinelike functions to perform.

Similarly, relations between Newtonian organizations are impersonal, rule-bound, or defined by formal contract, designed to exclude consideration of the idiosyncrasies or personalities of the entities with which they are contracting. If an oil company makes a contract to sell so many million gallons of fuel to an airline, it doesn't want to have to concern itself with whether the airline changes its CEO, or whether that CEO has an unfaithful wife or a sick child. Similarly, it is not the oil company's contractual concern whether the airline suffers a series of fatal crashes and goes bankrupt. That is what insurance is for.

The assumption in all Western, Newtonian organizational models is that the organization consists of separate parts bound together insofar as is necessary or desirable through universal rules or centralized control. Information flow and learning within such organizations is mediated through the negotiated, rule-bound structures that make up the organizations' internal and external contracts. If I want to inform my Newtonian colleagues of some decision I have made, or of some change in procedure, I should do so through proper channels. If I need to have a job done, I should seek assistance from a designated authority.

The advantage of goal-oriented, rule-bound Western or Newtonian organizations is that they can be efficient and reliable. Their clear boundaries make membership unambiguous. Every procedure and every role is specified and pinned down in its place. Every employee knows exactly what is expected every day—and what is not. So long as procedure is followed and proper channels used, information can flow smoothly to those parts of the organization where it is directed. But there are disadvantages. Just as rules don't accommodate exceptions easily, these organizations are inflexible. Turning them around to deal with the unexpected takes time and thorough reprogramming. Indeed, most procedures take a lot of time. As an Indian employee of Delhi's state power company complained, "Every time I want to spend $5, I have to fill out fifty pieces of paper and wait three months for clearance." And where proper channels or existing procedures don't cover the situation, such organizations can suffer a "learning disability"—as happens all the time in companies where one division has benefited from some new educational or consulting technique, or even from a "creative mistake," but no infrastructure exists for communicating this to other divisions.

The structural model for our Western, Newtonian organizations is the serial thinking process in the human brain. Like the separate parts of an organization, the brain's neural tracts consist of separate neurons firing one-on-one to other separate neurons. Each individual firing pattern is orchestrated by a program (a set of rules), and this in turn has been learned for the purpose of solving some problem. Those neurons not involved in the program for solving the problem in hand are superfluous to the process. If a new problem arises, the serial thinking process cannot handle it until supplied with an alteration to its program. Thus it is efficient and reliable, but rule-bound and therefore inflexible. On its own, serial thinking can't deal with complex data or rapid changes. Its neural circuits can deal only with a few inputs and outputs at any one time. This, for instance, is why PCs—modeled on serial thinking—can't deal with pattern recognition. Patterns are too complex.

In the human brain, serial thinking does not function in isolation. It is only in our mechanistic, cognitive-science models of thinking that it does so. Taking the structures of serial thinking alone as the central model for organizational structures is distorting the whole ball game. In the real brain, serial, parallel, and quantum (creative, insightful) thinking structures are integrated and work in tandem to generate our uniquely human thinking processes. In the same fashion, the uniquely complex human self functions as a dialogue between the public and private aspects of that self, however high the wall our distorted models of the self may build between the two.

The Newtonian universe, we know, is bound inexorably to the law of entropy. All those rule-bound, well-organized conglomerations of separate particles are destined to slow down and fall apart. All Newtonian systems are fated to certain death in a cold and silent universe. Yet complex, living systems manage to beat the odds. Real brains manage to rewire themselves throughout life. Both have their own dynamic of spiraling complexity, adaptation, and growth. Nature is telling us there is a better model for organizations than Newton's, a better model for thinking than rule-bound, goal-oriented thinking in isolation. "Management by objectives" may be a good model for management, but there are better models for leadership.

6

The Eastern Model:

The Networked Self and the Networked Organization

Chinese managers like to boast that, in contrast to their legalistic western peers, their businesses are based around negotiating relationships, not contracts. The chief assets of an overseas Chinese business are usually its guanxi (or connections).

–John Micklethwait and Adrian Wooldridge,
The Witch Doctors

I would like to begin with a tale of two conferences. I was invited to be a keynote speaker at each. The first was organized by a Western oil company and held in a large American city. I was told in advance what I was expected to speak about, for how long, and how much I would be paid. Three weeks before the conference opened I received a detailed agenda for the whole session, broken down into forty-five-minute segments punctuated here and there by lunches, break-out sessions, and coffee breaks, all of definite length. Each speaker was described and a tight résumé of the planned speech offered in advance. The thoughts that would be "processed" during each break-out session were specified. A pre-conference manual supplied every table and diagram to which speakers and facilitators would refer. The conference was supposed to be about transformation and out-of-the-box thinking!

The second conference was organized by a Japanese retailing billionaire and held in Kyoto. Vague, quasi invitations to speak had been arriving at my home for months before an actual date was finally set and a plane ticket offered. Two weeks before I was due to leave for Japan, I realized I knew nothing about the conference. What was I to speak about and for how long? To what size audience? Who else was speaking? What would I be paid? What was the conference *about?* In answer to my urgent fax putting these questions, the host's Korean assistant wrote back saying, "Don't concern yourself with these matters. This is going to be a Taoist conference. We will just all meet and see what emerges. We will have some good meals and make some good friendships. Then we will see what we can agree about." This conference has continued in peripatetic fashion for a year subsequently. The Japanese businessman, his Korean assistant, and I have dined together in three world capitals and continued to develop our friendship." I think they are concerned about the nature of the self and have some vague plans to institute a new form of education. The details have yet to emerge.

The Wavelike Self

The Japanese don't have a specific word for "self." They are concerned with relationships, and what we Westerners call the "self" is, for them, a matter of who is related to whom and in what larger social context. Nobel Prize-winning Japanese physicist Leo Esaki, who has spent his life working for IBM, compares Japanese society to a state of superfluid helium. Every particle is related to every other to such an extent that boundaries don't exist and the parts share the identity of the whole.

The Chinese sociologist Fei Xiaotong, as I wrote earlier, compares Confucian society to a complex pattern of interlocking waves, each fanning outward from some stone (individual) dropped in one of the many centers, but all so intricately involved that no clear boundary can be discerned between the waves caused by one stone and those of another. "Everyone stands at the center of the circles produced by his or her own social influence. Everyone's circles are interrelated. One touches different circles at different times and places."

In Confucian society, probably the purest example of the "Eastern model," the wave description of selfhood is at its most extreme opposite from our Western, particle model of the self. In Chinese culture, I am defined by my relationships, but I have many different kinds and circles of relationship and thus the boundaries of my own identity are quite ambiguous and contextual. With my parents I will have one way of conducting myself, with my children another, with my wider kinsfolk still another, with neighbors, members of my community, or my state still more. I can't state *the* set of moral principles that guides my life because I have many such sets of principles, each applicable in its own context. A Western notion of universal moral codes makes no sense in such societies.

"In these elastic networks that make up Chinese society," writes Fei, "there is always a self at the center of each web. But this notion of the self amounts to egocentrism, not individualism." In individualist, Western societies, the whole is made up of its parts and each part has its tightly defined identity circumscribed by boundaries. In its public aspect at least, every part (every individual) is equal to every other. Every individual has the same rights and obligations within an organization as anyone else with the same organizational status or function. In Chinese society, my self is always at the center of my circle, but I have many circles and the characteristics, obligations, and codes of each circle define who I am and how I should behave. I have no universal rights; only contextual obligations. Fei adds, "The boundary between public and private spheres is relative—we may even say ambiguous."

In the West, even my most private relationships are bound by contract. Some aspects of my behavior are bound by a specific contract, all other aspects are not. My obligations are limited by the terms and boundaries of the contract. In the Chinese networks consisting of circles within circles, there can be no hard-and-fast boundary to my obligations nor any limit to those relationships that might share my blame if I err. Improper conduct toward my mother-in-law reflects badly on the way my mother raised me, which reflects badly on the way her teachers and parents educated her, and so on. Everyone is responsible for everyone else. In the Introduction to *From the Soil,* Fei quotes this stark example from "The Myth of the 'Five Human Relations' of Confucius":

Cheng Han-cheng's wife had the insolence to beat her mother-in-law. This was regarded as such a heinous crime that the following punishment was meted out. Cheng and his wife were both skinned alive, in front of the mother, their skin was displayed by the city gates in various towns and their bones burned to ashes. Cheng's grand uncle, the eldest of his close relatives, was beheaded; his uncle and two brothers, and the head of the Cheng clan, were hanged. The wife's mother, her face tattooed with the words 'neglecting her daughters education', was paraded through seven provinces. Her father was beaten 80 strokes and banished to a distance of 3000 *li*. The heads of family in the houses to the right and left of the Chengs' were beaten 80 strokes and banished to Heilongjiang. The educational officer in the town was beaten 60 strokes and banished to a distance of 1000 *li*. Cheng's nine-month-old boy was given a new name and put in the county magistrate's care. Cheng's land was to be left in waste 'forever'. All this was recorded on a stone stele and rubbings of the inscriptions were distributed throughout the empire.

In the West, we wonder whether parents should be held at all responsible for the behavior of their delinquent children!

Waves and Organization

The Confucian model of the contextual, relational self is perhaps the most pure, as I said earlier. But throughout Asian societies, including India, this basically more wavelike model of self has underpinned group-oriented, networked, and most commonly family-based companies. Because Asian societies differ so much more among themselves in their social structures than Western ones, any hard-and-fast generalization comes unstuck. Japanese companies are very different in many respects from the large family networks of the overseas Chinese, and both are different from some of the star companies in Taiwan and Singapore. India has superimposed Western-style bureaucracy and management techniques in business onto an essentially networked, family-oriented society, not infrequently ending up with the worst of both worlds. But my purpose here is simply to draw a distinctive contrast between particle-like Western models of self and organization and wavelike Eastern models, regional variations notwithstanding.

Among the overseas Chinese, the networked self has formed the basis of large, complex, and ambiguous networked organizations very reminiscent of the neural networks found in the brain's parallel thinking structures. Like neural networks, everything and everyone seems to be connected to everything else. The connections within the networks are informal and pretty much organic—they grow in response to conditions, opportunities, and local constraints, much as neural network connections grow in response to experience. In this sense, both are flexible and adaptive. Both can learn. The size of the neuron bundles joined in a neural network varies with requirements, just as the ambiguous boundaries of family and kinship that underpin Chinese business networks expand and contract to suit needs.

On the downside, in both neural networks and Chinese networks, flexibility is limited through the crucial importance of habit, familiarity, and tradition. The brain's parallel connections function best with repeated experience. Chinese businesspeople are most comfortable with relations of trust, and the trust itself is reliable because of the tradition-bound nature of Chinese social relations. Stability in these communities is achieved through reinforced familiarity, custom, and discipline of the self. And they're a bit claustrophobic. "The more linkages one maintains," says Fei, "the more intensively one is wedged into an existing social order and is committed to the status quo." Thus where bureaucratic Western organizations can get fossilized by rules and procedures, networked Eastern organizations can be just as weak at dealing with unexpected change.

The brain's parallel processing structures—those used for tacit knowledge, skill acquisition, and pattern recognition—work cooperatively and locally. They are the structural prototype of agrarian societies and small groups anywhere in the world, groups that function well because everyone knows everyone else, most important knowledge is shared, responsibilities and necessary tasks are shared, and power is distributed according to tradition. Such societies need few formal rules because familiarity and the weight of group expectation keep most people in order.

As a young child in the early 1950s, I had personal experience with these close-knit groups. I was raised by my grandparents in a small country town in America's Midwestern farm belt. The town's population was only two hundred adults, all of whom worked in the local pickle factory, in the few local shops, or in jobs servicing local farms. Everyone in the town knew everyone else, knew their children and kept an eye on them, knew their health problems, their marital difficulties, their small scandals, their achievements, and their contributions to the community.

Both my grandparents belonged to a number of small groups that met in the town. Both belonged to the "True Blue Society" of the local church, the group for church members over fifty years old. My grandmother belonged to the local teachers' association and to the Ladies' Grange Society, a group of town and farm wives who met to plan local farm-centered events and to raise money for local charity. My grandfather belonged to the Elks and to the local branch of the Ohio Justices Association, a group formed by justices of the peace from nearby towns. Nearby, my great-grandfather was the ward chairman of the local Democratic Party, and a small group of party members met regularly in his sitting room. We all belonged, of course, to our own large, extended family, to the circle of my grandparents' fourteen siblings, their children, and grandchildren. All lived within a fifteen-mile radius of our town and some subgroup of us met at least once a week to spend Sundays and important family occasions together.

My grandparents and I were seldom alone in our house except when we slept. There was always a flow of townspeople or relatives meeting in our sitting room, gathered at the large kitchen table, or grouped around the bed to which my grandfather was confined much of the time with heart trouble. Our house and our lives seemed always at the center of the extended lives of the various groups who passed through and stayed awhile. There was constant, ongoing conversation (about local and national politics, about religion, about town events or town policies, about what the local grocery store should stock and what it was charging) that sometimes reached high-pitched argument but was always lively. My memories and the *meaning* of my childhood are inseparable from memories of all these people, their activities and conversation.

In the West, when people moved from small rural communities to large impersonal cities, a different social structure was imposed, and the small groups broke up. My parents' generation moved to the nearby city and took assembly-line jobs in factories. Church attendance and local-society memberships dropped off among family members, and so did our family get-togethers. Where my grandmother had belonged to an education association whose members never counted the hours or the energy they devoted to their teaching jobs, my mother joined a teachers' union and fought for better pay and conditions. Teaching became a job instead of a vocation. The cousins of my own generation then moved to other cities or other countries, wherever their jobs took them. I never see them, and I don't know their children's names. Rule-bound, bureaucratic organization and its imposed, impersonal mobility became the norm. The local and diverse meaning structures of the small groups and the small community to which my family had traditionally belonged were lost. Our personal lives are the poorer, but so are our working and political lives. Aspects of life that were all of a piece now happen in compartments.

Bureaucracy and rural, Eastern-style community life are by no means mutually exclusive. There was no society on earth more bureaucratic than the Confucian Chinese, and much of this survives today. But as China observers note, the difference between Western bureaucracy and Chinese bureaucracy is that we take it seriously, whereas the Chinese have found a million ways round it. If the Chinese want to get something done, they ignore the local functionary and go instead to the best friend of a fifth cousin twice removed.

Despite the durability of overseas Chinese business networks, observers wonder whether Western-style compartmentalization might not be the fate awaiting them in the modern world. The networks work stunningly well on a local scale, but can they translate their formula to large and complex global markets? Can Confucian family traditions and unquestioned respect for the authority of elders allow sufficient upward mobility for the talented and the challenging? Looking back to the brain's parallel thinking structures for a clue to answering such questions, I would think not. Neural networks can adapt sufficiently to recognize unfamiliar but *existing* patterns, but they cannot create *new* patterns. The ever-strengthening connections between neurons require the weight of habit, of repeated experience, that is, of familiarity. There is no place in a neural network for the maverick neuron that wants to experiment with some new sequence of firing. In consequence, the thinking generated by these networks is more inductive generalization than true insight. It doesn't give rise to new hypotheses or new paradigms like those found in the work of creative (maverick) geniuses like Copernicus, Beethoven, Nietzsche, or Edison.

Japanese companies have succeeded where Chinese networks may fail. There are countless instances of global Japanese corporations competing successfully in complex international markets. Indeed, they thrive on them. Yet the Japanese wavelike model of the self takes its toll on these companies as well. Decisions are taken (control exercised) not by dictatorial fiat, as in many of the Chinese family networks, but by consensus. That is the Japanese tradition. And consensus takes time. Consensus and concern with the good opinion of the group are also uncomfortable with difference, with the swashbuckling, maverick entrepreneur whose apparently mad ideas may bring about great leaps forward. Just as neural networks in the brain are best at small adaptations to existing structure, Japanese industry has made its fortune on clever adaptation of Western inventions. Even many of its successful management techniques were adaptations of Western ideas like those of Demming, where the Japanese genius was to see the applicability of something their more hidebound Western colleagues could not fit into the existing system. Their successful application of fuzzy logic was again a wise application to technology of a Western mathematical breakthrough that Western industry could not appreciate. It didn't fit the rules. But Japan still looks in vain for its own Bill Gates.

Western particle-like models of the self and Eastern wavelike models have thus given rise to quite different organizational structures, each with their own strengths and weaknesses. Like serial thinking structures in the brain, atomistic Western societies are individualist and rule-bound. They recognize a unique personal self, but regard it as isolated. The inevitability of conflict between so many independently functioning parts (individuals) is brought under control through formal rules and contracts, each of which has a universal quality—everyone is equal within the terms of the contract. Everyone has the same rights. A sharp division is made between the public and private aspects of the self, and organizational stability is assured through excluding the private, the turbulence of emotions and associations. Boundaries are rigid and organizations try to organize only those qualities that are predictable and thus controllable. Leadership of such organizations is mechanistic—straightforward command and control backed up by the authority of the rules.

The wavelike models of the self that predominate in the East, like neural networks in the brain, envision the self as wholly embedded in relationship. The emphasis is not on how to control conflict but rather on how to achieve cooperation. Boundaries between individuals and between the public and private spheres of individual identity are ambiguous, elastic. Thus networked organizations are more adaptive, expanding and contracting their boundaries, evolving their strategies in slow, organic stages. Control, or stability, is maintained through reinforced familiarity, custom, tradition, and self-discipline. Leadership style varies from one Asian culture to another, but the underlying basis of leadership is tradition, and therefore consensus.

In the brain, the serial and parallel thinking structures perform very different functions. The logical, rule-bound serial structures are necessary for practical, goal-oriented thinking. They make it possible for us to do mental arithmetic, to plan journeys from a timetable, or to devise a budget. The associative physical and emotional parallel structures handle tacit knowledge, skills, and patterns. But like both Western bureaucracies and Chinese networks, both rely on stability. Table 2 illustrates the differences and similarities. One is rule-bound, the other habit-bound. Both are weak at dealing with unexpected change. They seek to dampen down or to exclude the unexpected. And neither, on its own, is creative. Serial thinking works within an existing program; bureaucratic organizations work within the rules. Parallel thinking is reinforced through repeated experience. It recognizes *existing* patterns. Networked organizations rely on habit and tradition.

We have seen in earlier chapters that when our brain needs to rewire itself—when it needs to make a creative breakthrough, do some out-of-the-box thinking—a third kind of brain structure comes into play to integrate the other two. The brain's third kind of thinking suggests there may be available to us a third model of the self and a third model for organizational structures, a model that allows organizations to function at the creative edge. Based on quantum thinking, I want now to look at the quantum self and the quantum organization.

West	East
Conflict and control	Cooperation
Self (the personal) wholly excluded and isolated; interactions grounded in universal principles	Self (the personal) wholly embedded and contextual; no universal principles
Stability achieved through excluding the self and the emotions, and organizing only the predictable and controllable aspects of relationships	Stability achieved through reinforced familiarity and discipline of the self
Rigid boundaries	Ambiguous boundaries
Dictatorial leadership	Consensual leadership
Rule-bound	Habit-bound
Mechanical	Organic
Both	
Rely on stability	
Weak in dealing with unexpected change	
Seek to dampen down or exclude the unexpected	

Table 2. Self and Organization, West and East

7

The Quantum Model:

Bridging East and West

The idea of a quantum self is a new model of the self derived from the characteristics of the new science, particularly those of quantum physics. I believe this new model of self can transcend the divide between the classic Western and Eastern (or rural) models and can underpin a new theory of organization and leadership.

The nature of human consciousness and human creativity is at the cutting edge of scientific inquiry today. The majority of mainstream cognitive scientists still believe that both will ultimately be explained in mechanistic terms. We have, they say, a "mind machine" inside our heads. One day, they believe, we will have computing machines that can do anything we can do, probably better and faster. But there is another school of scientific thought that believes human consciousness can never be mimicked by machines. *In principle*, they say, mind is not machinelike. These scientists look for the origins of consciousness and creativity in brain processes not described by Newton's physics.

Many believe these more creative mental processes are quantum in origin, that quantum physics literally makes possible the characteristics of the human self—humor, grief, relationship, creativity, a sense of meaning, understanding, free will, loyalty, commitment, and so on.

Personally, as I discussed at length in my earlier book, *The Quantum Self*, I back quantum theories of mind. But these theories are still speculative, and we needn't wait for the scientific evidence to come in.

Our purpose here is to find a new conceptual structure for organizations. Quantum physics provides that for two good reasons. It offers a radically new way to think about the problems and opportunities confronting organizations and their need for new infrastructures. And, for whatever reason, human consciousness and creativity do behave like processes described by the new science. There is an uncanny similarity between quantum events and our more creative mental events.

So far, we have seen two diametrically opposed models of the self and their effect on organizations. The particle model of the self, so important to Western management theory, is modeled on Newtonian science. This Newtonian self, like the science that inspired it, is seen as atomistic, determined in its behavior, fragmented into separate parts circumscribed by rigid boundaries, and isolated from its environment. Newtonian organizations are rule-bound, they exclude private, unpredictable aspects of the self, they divide functions and structures, and they, too, are isolated from their environment. These organizations function very like the brain's one-on-one neural tracts, which give us logical, rational, rule-bound, how-to thinking. This is our "first kind of thinking." It gives us our "mental intelligence."

The Eastern, wave model of the self, lying at the heart of networked Asian organizations (and small rural communities worldwide), is modeled on the complex patterns made by countless intersecting waves. Like waves, the networked self is seen as essentially relational and contextual. A person *is* his or her relationships. The boundaries of this self are elastic and ambiguous, and relationships between selves are governed by local custom, habit, and tradition. Networked organizations rely on personal contact and personal bonds, trust instead of rules. They make little or no distinction between the public and private spheres of life, they are complex in structure, and they learn from and adapt to their environment through trial and error. Networked organizations function very like the brain's neural networks, which give us tacit knowledge and the ability to learn skills and to recognize patterns. This is our "second kind of thinking." It gives us our bodily "emotional intelligence."

In the brain, as we have seen, logical (serial) thinking and networked (parallel) thinking are integrated through a third kind of neural function—synchronous neural oscillations binding different parts of the brain. This gives us our intuitive, insightful, creative thinking, the kind of thinking with which we challenge our assumptions and change our mental models. The kind of thinking with which we radically rewire our brains. This third kind of thinking gives us our "spiritual intelligence," our intelligence rooted in meaning, vision, and value. It allows us to use our whole brains. I have argued that organizations need it (need infra-structures that make it possible) to use their whole brains. We need it to rewire the corporate brain.

I've called our third kind of thinking *quantum thinking* because of its similarity to quantum processes. I want now to use the central features of quantum processes to discover features of a quantum self. Then we can discuss how to organize and lead quantum selves in a quantum organization.

Features of the Quantum Self

Quantum science, indeed all the new sciences, describe a physical world that is holistic, indeterminate or at least unpredictable, and self-organizing. Quantum systems are particle-like and wavelike at the same time, they have both individual and group properties. They are governed by the Uncertainty Principle, which thrives on ambiguity, yet when we focus on or measure them we can pin them down precisely. Unlike isolated Newtonian systems, quantum systems are always in and part of each other and their environment; quantum observers are always part of what they observe. Quantum observers evoke, or cocreate, reality.

We human beings are physical systems, too, and fully part of the physical world. Our bodies, certainly, and most likely our minds, obey the same laws as everything else in this universe. At the moment, the best physics we have for describing this universe is quantum physics. "I," ultimately, am a quantum system. As such, my self should have the following qualities:

• *The quantum self is both-and.* It has both a unique, particle-like individual aspect and a shared, relational, wavelike group aspect. I am me, my genes, my history, and my unique experience, but I am also all those others with whom I live and work and share experience and to whom I relate. Neither my private, individual self nor my public, relational self is more important or more primary. Both are just facts, and to be interesting and to be used for my own and my community's maximum benefit, they must be integrated. A quantum society would have infrastructures that nourish both the private self and the public self, and which allow them to nourish each other.

• *The quantum self is holistic and contextual.* The wavelike, relational boundaries of the quantum self extend, in principle, across the universe. My self is interwoven with and defined by everything else that exists. I am in nature, nature is in me. I am a part of all others, and all others are a part of me. I am not just my brother's keeper. I am my brother. I am not just a natural system, but natural systems are affected by me, and I by them. My body is made out of star-dust; my mind emerges in dialogue with the four forces of the universe and the laws that define them. It may be a further natural force. Even my particle-like inner boundaries change, adapt, and re-form in dialogue with my environment and my experience. My genes themselves are active or inactive in different environments. My self is integrated and dynamic, each part, each subself or subpersonality, affected by and affecting every other. I am a whole chorus of conversations in harmony.

• *The quantum self is self-organizing.* It is at the edge, poised precariously and yet creatively between order and chaos. The quantum self has no hard limits, no set, definable boundaries. It has constraints (such as the force of habit), but it is not determined. It has a genetic code, but this is always choosing what parts of itself to express. It has a character, but this is always being molded. The quantum self is always reinventing itself, always rewiring its brain. "I" am a dynamic pattern, an open, dynamic system, a whirlpool. I have no soul in the sense of some little box inside me or some discrete part of my brain that can be registered on a CAT or a PET scan. My soul is a continually self-organizing process, a channel between me and the ground state of reality. It is expressed through all of me, through my thoughts, my emotions, my bodily feelings, and my body language. All of me and all of my experience has a soulful, a sacred, dimension. This includes my work experience.

• *The quantum self is free.* It is constrained but not determined by any genetic material, by any past experience, by any environmental conditions or conditioning, or by any given neural wiring in its brain. The self's boundaries are elastic and in flux, subject to a creative uncertainty.

Its neural connections are constantly being rejiggered and wired anew. The quantum self is an active agent in the world, not a passive victim. It is a self that chooses, and through its choices it chooses itself and its environment.

• *The quantum self is responsible.* It is in and part of the world with which it interacts. The quantum self lives in a participatory universe and it actively participates in the unfolding of that universe. It is an active agent of reality, a cocreator. The questions that I ask, the thoughts that I think, the emotions and fantasies that I harbor, the decisions that I make, and the actions I take mold the world and others around me. I am a stone dropped into a pond that sends ripples outward in every direction. I am the world. If that world is to be a different place, it is because I will make it different. If something needs to be created, I must act as midwife to its creation. The buck stops here.

• *The quantum self is spiritual.* It is steeped in meaning, vision, and value. The quantum self is an excitation of the underlying quantum vacuum, a ripple on the pond that represents the ground state of reality. The quantum vacuum is the soul of the universe, the "mind of God," and each quantum self is a thought in the mind of God. Each self represents one of nature's, or God's, potentialities, one of the many infinite paths from A to B. I have a destiny, a necessity to ask questions of meaning about my path and a need to be driven by meaning. I am fated always to ask, Why? and What for? and Couldn't it be otherwise? and to seek and to create answers.

These are the features of the self that a quantum organization must nourish and harness. These are the needs and potentialities for which there must be corporate infrastructures in any organization that wants to use all of its human potential and all of its brain. Indeed, as we shall see, in some fashion or other these qualities of the quantum self are qualities that a quantum organization must itself possess.

Eight Features of a Quantum Organization

In Chapter Three, I applied eight principles of the new science to leadership. I think those same principles can give us the basic thinking we need to see the most important characteristics of a quantum organization. Each organizational feature also suggests infrastructures that can employ the full potentialities of the quantum self and of quantum thinking. These are infrastructures that should assist flexible and creative adaptation to new global, societal, and market potentialities and enable organizations to thrive on ambiguity and rapid change. Let's briefly review the eight main features of the new science, and apply them to organizations.

1. The new science is holistic. The whole organizes the parts and every part is related to and partially defined through every other part. In quantum physics, relationship helps to create further facts, new realities. Events always happen in a context.

• *The quantum organization is holistic.* Most large corporate organizations now find themselves in a global context. Even more local ones realize that small shifts within local markets or local societies are felt throughout the world. Stock market jitters in Tokyo are reflected in London and New York within hours. Drought conditions in one South American country affect coffee prices worldwide. The manufacturing processes of individual industries depend upon environmental conditions and natural resources. In turn they have a direct and lasting effect on the global environment. The success or failure of any one company depends upon the activities, successes, and failures of other companies, never mind those of political systems and national economies. The corrupt behavior of a few corporate individuals can ruin millions of lives and destabilize international institutions.

Mechanistic notions that the corporate world consists of isolated units each ruthlessly pursuing its own self-interest cannot cope with this interlinkage. Neither can a model of the individual corporation that divides itself into isolated divisions and functions set to compete against each other. Cobbled together out of separate, uncoordinated parts and yet impinged upon from every direction, mechanistic systems have become unwieldy and unstable. Old models of conflict and confrontation must give way to new models of dynamic integration. These must protect the integrity of individual concerns while drawing them into a larger working whole.

The quantum organization will have infrastructures that encourage and build on relationships, relationships between leaders and employees, between employees and their colleagues, between divisions and functional groups, between structures themselves. It will also be aware of its environmental context, human, corporate, societal, and ecological, and will build infrastructures that encourage exchange and dialogue with these. Nothing is really too far afield to be outside the corporate brief.

2. Quantum and complex systems are indeterminate or at least unpredictable. They are poised at the edge between order and chaos, between particle-like states and wavelike states, between actuality and potentiality. Their indeterminacy makes them flexible, ready to evolve in any direction.

• *The quantum organization must be flexible and responsive, at the edge.* Ambiguity, complexity, and rapid change increasingly dominate events both inside and outside the corporation. The corporate environment is evolving—and so must the corporation. Shifting boundaries of responsibility and identity, experimental modes of living and working, new information sources and new technological systems all demand flexible response. Mechanistic patterns of fixed functional or individual roles and rigidly organized structures for management and control inhibit the potential latent in human response, imagination, and organization.

The infrastructures of a quantum organization should be like a blend of waves and particles. They should be like movable walls, like the Volvo car-building team desks on wheels. They can rest in one place when needed, but can also move. Quantum infrastructures should be less like constructions made out of Mechano or even Lego and more like plasticine, which can take any shape and be changed at will. Quantum infrastructures can adapt to the shifting and sometimes contradictory needs of individuals and teams, the corporate need to be sometimes mechanistic and sometimes organic, the complementary and sometimes conflicting need to be both local and global, both competitive and cooperative.

3. The new science is emergent and self-organizing. The newly emergent whole constructed through relationship is always greater than the sum of its parts. Chaotic and quantum systems are creative, always generating surprise and increased complexity.

• *The quantum organization must be bottom-up, self-organizing, and emergent.* There is the potentiality for something deeply radical in new corporate thinking. We have seen the limitations of heavy, top-down hierarchies and structures of control imposed by theory, tradition, or boardroom authority. They are inflexible in the face of change and waste the creative, spontaneous resources of the quantum self.

The infrastructures of the quantum organization must nourish human and organizational creativity. They must enhance inner mobility and personal responsibility and facilitate the free flow of information and ideas. There must be spaces in the organization without boundaries, relationships without fear. The parts (whether individuals, teams, functions, or divisions) must be free to rearrange themselves. Some decision making must be relocated among front-line workers and front-line managers. (As a Volvo manager told me, "We didn't know what we would get from the teams until we had the teams. But they worked!")

4. The new science is both-and rather than either-or. Matter consists of waves *and* particles, and has the potentialities of each. Quantum systems follow many paths from A to B; adaptive evolution proceeds through multiple mutation.

• *The quantum organization will thrive on diversity.* The old vision of one truth, one way, one expression of reality, one best way of doing things, the either-or of absolute, unambiguous choice must give way to a plural way of accommodating the multiplicities and diversities of societies, markets, and individuals. Either-or must make way for both-and. "My way" must give way to shared vision, shared opportunity, and shared responsibility that recognize the validity of many paths from A to B. As Einstein said, there are as many perspectives on the universe as there are observers, and each adds something.

A quantum organization will have infrastructures that mix levels of responsibility, adapt to assorted educational, professional, and functional backgrounds, and decentralize power and decision making—infrastructures that really do "let a thousand flowers bloom" and never bring out the pruning shears of ideological purity. Diversity will not be imposed through mechanistic, politically correct appointments and directives, but through infrastructures that create a climate of dialogue.

5. Heisenberg's Uncertainty Principle tells us that when we interfere with a quantum system, we change it. When we structure an experiment, we influence the results. The questions we ask partially determine the answers we get.

• *A quantum organization would be like a jazz jam session.* In a symphony orchestra, each player concentrates on one instrument and one segment of the score, and the conductor constructs the whole out of these parts. Conductors' interpretations differ, and thus so can the sound of an identical symphony played by different orchestras, but the whole is always the sum of its parts, and the essential score doesn't change. In a jazz jam session, players are often expert at different instruments, and there is no set score and no conductor. There is an evolving background theme, an emergent whole that organizes the parts, but the composite sound is always a surprise.

Newtonian companies create roles and sell products. Both roles and products are like a musical score that constrains production and dictates infrastructures. Goal-directed thinking, if successful, achieves its goal—but seldom anything more. Managers or consultants who assign tasks, if successful, get those tasks performed—but never know what else individuals or the organization might have achieved. A quantum organization would create infrastructures where different questions can be asked, different goals considered, different products or functions imagined. Roles would be less fixed, employees encouraged to play different instruments and to experiment with the score. A quantum leader would see himself as holding the space where the background theme can emerge. Quantum selves are designed to thrive at the edge. A quantum organization would have some infrastructures that allow the free play of uncertainty.

6. The new science has discovered that much that is interesting or valuable or creative about systems lies beyond the present moment, beyond our immediate grasp, and is waiting to unfold. Complex patterns called strange attractors lie sleeping within chaos. The goal toward which a quantum system evolves has yet to emerge. Both quantum and chaos science are about potentiality more than actuality, about the what might be rather than the what is. The new science dares to dream. It is playful.

• *A quantum organization would be playful.* Our tightly structured, results-oriented organizations are so serious, so frightened of failure. They want successes they can measure, successes they can predict. But neither nature nor children learn that way. Nature evolves through lots of mistakes. Most mutations are a mess. Ninety-nine percent of all species that have existed no longer exist. Nonlinear systems have to run through chaos before breaking through to complexity. Children play, and learn by mistakes. They take risks, but they don't even see them as such. When a young child builds a tower of bricks and it falls down, the child laughs with delight. Not because children love destruction, but because the child has learned something from the catastrophe. The next tower will benefit, and so will the child's brain. That's how it wires itself. When asked why he had so many creative ideas, the twice Nobel Prize-winning scientist Linus Pauling replied, "Oh, I just have a *lot* of ideas. Some of them are good."

A quantum organization would have infrastructures that encourage play and reward structures that recognize the value of taking risks. It might offer awards for the wildest idea or the most creative mistake of the week. It would recognize the value of wasted time or unstructured time, of nondirective conversations, of long lunches and faces gazing into space, of dream time.

7. Quantum physics describes a participatory universe. The observer is part of the observed reality. The observer is a cocreator who helps to make that reality happen.

• *A quantum organization would be "deeply green."* Ecologists recognize a difference between normal ecology and "deep ecology." Normal ecology worries about the earth's natural environment. Deep ecology interests itself in the earth as a total system, a system with a human, meaning-centered dimension that is in symbiosis with its nonhuman but life-centered dimension. A quantum organization would be deeply ecological about its environment. It would be concerned with its human environments, internal and external, and with its societal, cultural, and natural environments. Mechanism assumes a sharp dichotomy between human beings and the rest of creation, between culture and nature. Newtonian organizations use their environment, they exploit their resources, both human and natural. The quantum vision is different.

Just as the quantum self is in nature and nature is in the quantum self, a quantum organization lives and breathes its environment. It is in and of its environment. It accepts responsibility for its own cocreation of that environment—for the cocreation of its people, its surrounding society, the global community and global values, and the earth's environment. Quantum organizations would consider the importance of "deeply green" questions: What is work for? Do individuals exist to serve corporations and economies, or do corporations and economies exist to serve individuals? Business leaders are world leaders. And quantum leaders know that they make the world they live in.

8. Quantum field theory tells us that every existing thing is an excitation of the quantum vacuum. That is, it tells us that every existing thing is but one actual expression of the universe's manifold, infinitely unfolding potentiality. The quantum vacuum is the vision at the heart of the universe, and existing things exist to give birth to aspects of that vision.

• *A quantum organization will be vision centered and value driven.* A Newtonian organization sells products. It does its best to meet present demand or to manipulate demand, to manipulate public and market taste to want its products. It tries to create situations of scarcity, situations of discontent. It feeds on modern society's illusion that personal and spiritual emptiness can be filled with *things.* Often the market fails or ceases to respond. The customers become jaded, the company that tries to reach them fails.

A quantum organization would recognize that people seek meaning, that we transcend our frustrations and our limitations with dreams. Living systems are evolutionary systems, always reaching beyond themselves to new possibility. Customers want to envision new possibilities. A quantum organization would seek to give its customers possibilities, dreams, and meaning. Not cynically, like the worst of the ad men, but genuinely because the leaders of quantum organizations are themselves driven by deep vision and a need for meaning. (They are *servant leaders,* as described in Chapter Nine.) Such leaders encourage infrastructures that bring the private, meaning-centered side of their own and their employees' lives together with the public, work-centered and goal-oriented sides.

Coca-Cola has been selling much the same product for nearly a century. McDonald's hamburgers are the same in every city and every culture. But neither company is selling consumable items. Both are selling dreams. Coca-Cola used to sell the dream of the stable American family of the 1950s, with all its members secure in their roles and their material prosperity. Today Coca-Cola sells wind in your hair and rain on your face, raw sensuality, the feeling of being at the edge. McDonald's sells the American way of life for each culture to interpret in its own way. Virgin

West	East	Quantum
Conflict and control	Cooperation	Dialogue
Self (the personal) wholly excluded and isolated; interactions grounded in universal principles	Self (the personal) wholly embedded and contextual; no universal principles	Self (the personal) embedded and contextual with universal dimension
Stability achieved through excluding the self and the emotions, and organizing only the predictable and controllable aspects of relationships	Stability achieved through reinforced familiarity and discipline of the self	Stability balanced with instability
Rigid boundaries	Ambiguous boundaries	Flexible boundaries
Dictatorial leadership	Consensual leadership	Leader relies on trust and feel for situation
Rule-bound	Habit-bound	No set framework from rules or habits
Mechanical	Organic	Both naturally unfolding (organic) and that which can be made from it (mechanical)
Both		
Rely on stability		
Weak in dealing with unexpected change		Open to change
Seek to dampen down or exclude the unexpected		Thrives on unexpected

Table 3.   Self and Organization, West, East, and Quantum

sells youth and iconoclasm. British Telecom sells communication. Volvo sells Scandinavian solidity more than cars.

Dreams and visions can evolve in dialogue with the culture. They can adapt to needs and aspirations. Or they can tap deeply into those levels of human meaning and value that transcend culture and the aspirations of the moment. An organization that can channel these can both creatively adapt to and cocreate taste and need.

At the end of the last chapter, I offered a chart comparing the features of the Western model of self and organization with those of the Eastern model. I confess I like summing things up in charts. It helps to organize my thinking. So in Table 3 I have compared the features of all three models we have discussed—Western, Eastern, and quantum.

Many of the qualities I have listed in the preceding pages as features of a quantum organization are familiar. Business change agents have been talking about some of them for years. But they seldom come about. I hope that by describing them within the context of the coherent conceptual framework offered by the new science, they take on some added power to shift corporate thinking.

Practicing Quantum Insight

I don't know of any perfect, existing quantum organizations. Perhaps they are an idea, an archetype or an ideal toward which we can strive and through which we might improve on the present state of things. But there are some well-known organizations that have definite quantum features, organizations that have incorporated (sometimes consciously, sometimes not) quantum insights in their infrastructures and styles of leadership. Throughout this book I have referred to the Marks & Spencer example. Here, I want briefly to discuss two others.

VOLVO'S CAR-MAKING TEAMS

I discussed these Volvo teams a bit in Chapter Four. They were an experiment in response to a challenge.

Volvo production lines had for years been turning out cars that looked similar externally, but internally were very different. Few components were universal. This situation kept production costs high, and limited market appeal. The ideal, the company came to feel, would be just the opposite, to produce a wide range of cars that looked different externally, but shared many internal components. They felt that getting engineers from different functions to work on teams would be the answer.

The mechanistic work model that Volvo earlier considered was hierarchical and highly structured. Assign people to different groups, give each group a clear task and clear set of boundaries, and have all the groups supervised from above as in Figure 8. This model assumed the company already knew the detailed need for and outcome of each group.

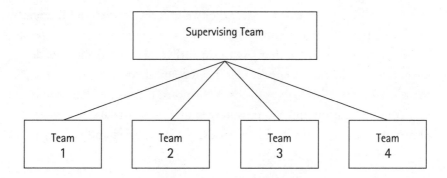

Figure 8.   Volvo's Original Hierarchical Model

After exploring both internal and external experiences, doing some reading on quantum physics and other new science theories, and reflecting on the unstructured or loosely structured nature of companies being run successfully by what some Volvo executives call the "Nintendo generation," the management had a learning breakthrough. They saw the learning and evolutionary value of uncertainty, of saying "I don't know," of taking risks, and they wanted to design infrastructures that could support these. The first step was envisioning a new learning model and beginning action on a small scale, as illustrated in Figure 9.

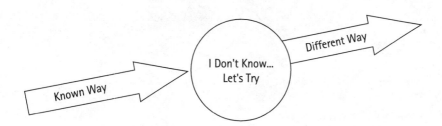

Figure 9.   Volvo's New Quantum Learning Model

With this learning model in mind, those with the task of designing the new teams drew what they privately refer to as "some quantum circles." They conceived twelve team modules, one for each of twelve crucial design features—chassis, seats, steering, and so on—of their various models. Engineers who once worked on different models within different functions, and who thus had a loyalty to diverse components, were now out together on teams and asked to conceive universal components. Smaller teams were formed within the twelve larger teams, and members of both large and small teams were given the freedom to move from one circle or subcircle to another. As I said earlier, even parts of their desks were put on wheels. No supervisory head team directs the various teams. Instead, a team of managers keeps the team of teams together by ensuring communication and a common overall vision of goals and concepts. The whole thing—sketched in Figure 10—is dynamic and self-organizing. And it works.

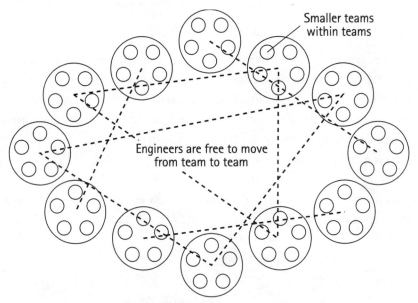

Figure 10. The Volvo Circles of Circles within Circles

VISA'S FEDERALISM

Dee Hock used to be a vice president at a Seattle bank that licensed Bank Americard, one of the world's earliest credit cards. Bank Americard was successful at first, but an ensuing credit card orgy driven by competing banks led to financial chaos. Bank of America held a crisis meeting of its licensees, the result of which was a committee set up to find a better model. Dee Hock was made chairman of the committee, and both the method he conceived for arriving at a new model and many features of that new model itself are quantum. They were inspired by the new science, by chaos theory and biological systems. Hock is fascinated by these concepts, and he writes and speaks prolifically about the development of Visa and their effect on it. The information and quotes cited here appeared in the October-November 1996 issue of *Fast Company Magazine*, "The Trillion Dollar Vision of Dee Hock," by M. Mitchell Waldrop.

Hock felt the first step toward developing a new credit card model had to be vision, getting the vision right. "Unless we can define a purpose for this organization that we can believe in, we might as well go home. . . . Far better than a precise plan is a clear sense of direction and compelling beliefs. And that lies within you. The question is, how do you evoke it?" His committee spent over a year just on this issue. Any company that Hock has touched since must go through a similar initial and prolonged dialogue phase. (See Chapter Eight.) As MIT's Peter Senge describes it, Hock uses that period of dialogue to "blow up the whole organization, dissolving power relationships, everything."

In conceiving Visa, Hock felt that there had to be a working balance between competition and cooperation. The new credit card would be issued globally by myriad local banks, each of which would want to serve its own customers with competitive terms and conditions. At the same time, the card had to be a global currency, with certain universal features available only through cooperation. I call this giving the organization particle-like (local) and wavelike (universal) features. Dee Hock calls it "chaordic," poised between chaos (competition) and order (cooperation).

Hock wanted the Visa organization to be "invisible," its structures so flexible that no one could "tell who owns it, where it's headquartered, how it's governed, or where to buy shares." He conceived a nonhierarchical, bottom-up power structure modeled on the American federal system. As M. Mitchell Waldrop describes it in *Fast Company* magazine,

> The organization must be adaptable and responsive to changing conditions, while preserving overall cohesion and unity of purpose. . . . The governing structure must not be a chain of command, but rather a framework for dialogue, deliberation, and coordination among equals. Authority, in other words, comes from the bottom up, not the top down. The U.S.

federal system is designed so authority rises from the people to local, state and federal governments; in Visa, which contains elements of the federal system, the member banks send representatives to a system of national, regional and international boards. While the system appears to be hierarchical, the Visa hierarchy is not a chain of command. Instead, each board is supposed to serve as a forum for members to raise common issues, debate them, and reach some kind of consensus and resolution.

In the language of this book, that is a quantum vision of the networked organization.

8

Dialogue:

A Chance to Grow New Neural Connections

So far, this has been a book largely about thinking, and about using new thinking to rewire the corporate brain. But using implies doing. It requires actions and tools for action. If a corporation wants to think and operate at the edge, it needs some methodology or infrastructure for doing so. Dialogue is such a method. Properly understood and practiced, the dialogue process and the dialogue group are a practical tool with which companies can make the transition from old thinking to new being and doing. Even the decision to undertake the dialogue process can change the way a company operates. The medium is the message.

I have spoken of dialogue many times throughout the previous chapters. We've seen that different neural systems of the brain are in dialogue with each other to give us the full benefit of our three kinds of thinking. I've spoken of dialogue within companies like Marks & Spencer and Motorola as a management technique, and of the necessity for dialogue between the divisions and power levels of organizations, between organizations, and between organizations and their wider environment. We certainly need dialogue between the various models of self and organization we have just discussed. But what is this stuff called *dialogue?*

The word dialogue is familiar to most of us. Too familiar, because it is used in so many ways to mean so many different things. Most people think they engage in dialogue whenever they engage in conversation, or at least whenever they have a good discussion or a good debate. Dialogue means "talking things through." But I mean something more specific by the word. I want to describe dialogue as an important and very particular process of our thinking and a powerful means by which we can grow new neural connections. I think it is a quantum process, a means of doing and using quantum thinking. Used in a corporate context, dialogue can be a crucial infrastructure for any thinking or learning organization, an infrastructure through which the corporate brain can rewire itself continuously. Some corporations use it already.

The history of dialogue is important. Its origins go back to ancient Athens. It was the main teaching method used by Socrates, the method immortalized in Plato's famous dialogues. The word dialogue itself is Greek, coming from *dia* and *logos*. *Dia* means "through" or "by way of." *Logos* has traditionally been translated as *word*, so *dia-logos* would mean "through words," "through talking." But there is an earlier and more original Greek meaning of *logos*. This is translated as *relationship*. *Dia-logos* is "through relationship." This gives the word a radically different and far more powerful meaning, particularly when we remember the creative importance of relationship in quantum science. Imagine *logos* translated in the Bible as *relationship:* "In the beginning was relationship."

In ancient Athens, dialogue was the special relationship between Socrates and his students. It was a form of ongoing conversation in which Socrates would teach people through asking them a seemingly endless series of questions. Each question was intended to undercut some assumption or prejudice or false belief in the student's last answer. Socrates believed that all human beings are born knowing everything, but that life is a process of forgetting. Truth, then, for him was unforgetting or "recalling" what we have always known, coming into possession of our original wisdom. The most famous instance of this Socratic dialogue technique used for unforgetting is in Plato's dialogue *The Meno*. Here, Socrates takes an ignorant slave boy wholly without education, and through a series of questions, elicits from him all the principles of higher mathematics. "See," comments Socrates, "he really knew it all along."

Dialogue was also a special relationship among the citizens of the city, enabling them to resolve their differences. Whenever there was an important issue to be considered, the citizens would meet in the *agora,* the marketplace, and hold a dialogue about it—for hours, for days if necessary, until they had seen some way through. This allowed the emergence of collective insight, collective wisdom, and a nonconfrontational way of solving problems. But then, as the years passed, the citizens of Athens became too numerous and too busy to engage in dialogue. So they hired paid advocates to put their positions and they voted on the advocates' arguments. Dialogue was replaced with debate. Democracy became a focus on voting between set positions instead of a relationship allowing many positions and new insight to emerge.

Ever since the appearance of those paid advocates in ancient Athens, debate has been our familiar Western form of solving disagreements or arriving at decisions. We think the presence of heated debate is the sign of a healthy democracy. We teach the art of debate in our schools and look for it in our politicians. It has become the central model for most conversation between individuals and within groups in Western societies. I think debate is a particularly Newtonian, mechanistic form of conversation. It is about the conflict of ideas and the confrontation between their advocates, like the clash between those steel balls in the "Newton's Cradle" toy. We even use the expression "Let's bounce some ideas off each other." Public debates are formal, constrained by rules and boundaries and accepted speaking techniques.

Debate and Dialogue

We can look at some contrasting features of debate and dialogue to see what radically different approaches they are to conversation and relationship. The difference is important to corporate thinking. It certainly has wider societal and educational implications.

KNOWING VERSUS FINDING OUT

In a debate, I know which position I am advocating or defending. I know the main points of my argument and—if well prepared—know the most clever way to present them. I know my position is right. Debate is clever, it is cerebral. I do it with my head.

137

Dialogue is about finding out, about discussing something openly until I break through to some new knowledge or insight. I might go to a dialogue knowing what I think is the case, but I am willing to suspend my certainty and listen to the discussion with an open mind. And with an open heart. Dialogue involves my emotions and my deeper sensitivities, as well as my best intellectual thinking faculties.

ANSWERS VERSUS QUESTIONS

In a debate, because I know, I have all the answers. You have nothing to teach me. I am here to teach you, or to convince you, or to defeat you. I talk at you.

Dialogue is about questions, about the things I don't know or the things I would like to find out. It's about exploration—of myself, of the other, of the matter at hand. Why do these words make me feel angry or anxious? Why have you said that? Where are you coming from? What is your point of view and why do you hold it? Is that possibly another way to look at things? What assumptions have I been harboring? Where has my point of view been coming from? What is my paradigm?

WINNING OR LOSING VERSUS SHARING

In a debate, somebody knows, somebody has the answers, and the other person is wrong. So one us will win and the other will lose. One point of view will be judged better than the other, one line of argument best. There is one best way from A to B and we'll vote on that.

Dialogue is about sharing. We share our points of view, we share our assumptions, our doubts and uncertainties, our questions, our fears, our suggestions and wild ideas. We propose as many paths from A to B as we can jointly imagine and we consider them together. We *feel* them together.

UNEQUAL VERSUS EQUAL

Debate is unequal because one of us is right and one of us is wrong. One of us will win and the other must lose. One of us has the answers, the other is in error. One point of view will be judged better than the other. We will choose, or the audience will choose.

Somebody has been more clever, more eloquent, more entertaining.

Dialogue is equal because we all have something to contribute. Unless a person is insane, he or she has some valid reason for holding a point of view or harboring a feeling. There is something valid about any point of view or any feeling any of us may entertain. There are no wrong points of view, no invalid ways to feel. I am here to learn your reasons and your feelings and to understand their origins. And to understand my own response to them.

POWER VERSUS RESPECT OR REVERENCE

Debate is about power. My power to defeat you or to win you over or to make you compromise. My power to persuade you or to make you look like a fool.

Dialogue is about respect. My respect for your point of view and how you have arrived at it, my respect for your feelings, for your contribution. It may even be about reverence. My gratitude to you for seeing things differently than I do, my reverence for your different personality, your different history, your different experience, your ability to enrich me with them. Each of us can only express one of life's (reality's) many possibilities. I revere your showing me there are others, revere your making those others possible.

Debate versus Dialogue

Debate	Dialogue
Knowing	Finding out
Answers	Questions
Winning or losing	Sharing
Unequal	Equal
Power	Respect or reverence
Proving a point; defending a position	Listening; exploring new possibilities

Note: Dialogue is not necessarily about reaching consensus.

PROVING A POINT VERSUS LISTENING

Debate is about proving a point or defending a position. I attack you and I build defenses against you, against your point of view. I close myself to you and your words and your feelings. I don't want to know.

Dialogue is about exploring new possibilities. It is about listening. In dialogue I create a space inside myself where I can hear you, where I can feel what you are saying. I create a space inside myself where I can hear myself, where I can listen to and feel my own reactions to what you say. Most of us are not very good at listening. Our experience and our education have prepared us to be always ready with a thought or a reaction or a good argument. This overpreparedness blocks out what we might learn or hear. It makes us deaf. And insensitive—insensitive to others and to ourselves.

Dialogue in Itself

Like good quantum thinking, dialogue makes us surface and challenge our assumptions. It leads us to change our existing mental models. It is a structure that dissolves previous structures.

Dialogue is not necessarily about reaching consensus. Our Western culture teaches us there is one best way, one best point of view, one God, one Truth. Ideally, we should all be able to agree about this. The convergence of all differences toward one cozy agreement is our cultural ideal, the end and goal of Western history. We fear difference, we resist the possibility that two people might disagree and yet both might be right. We can't handle that.

There is a famous Sufi story about the Mullah Nasruddin. Nasruddin was a wise man or a fool, depending on your point of view. In this particular story, two men have come to the mullah with an argument. The first man puts his case, and Nasruddin says, "I perceive that you are right." Then the second man puts his own, contradictory case, and once again Nasruddin says, "I perceive that *you* are right." A third man looking on objects. How can Nasruddin say that both men are right when they entirely disagree? To him Nasruddin says, "I perceive that you also are right."

The Mullah Nasruddin, like Socrates, was a practitioner of dialogue. In my own experience, some of the best dialogue groups I have ever attended have ended with nobody agreeing with anybody else. Yet everyone has emerged enriched. Dialogue is about that enrichment. It is a celebration of difference. It is about what we can learn from difference and the wisdom of knowing that truth isn't always simple. It's about knowing that human nature and human situations and human problems are not simple and that if there are any solutions, these, too, are seldom simple.

The concept of dialogue lay dormant in Western culture for centuries. In the 1940s, the practice was revived by the group psychology movement as a new approach to group discussion and conflict resolution. In the 1970s, the quantum physicist David Bohm took up the cause of dialogue. Bohm saw that it was a particularly quantum approach to conversation and he felt it could be used to change society. Through Bohm's work, dialogue began to spread. It was taken up by the MIT Learning Center and featured widely in Peter Senge's best-selling *The Fifth Discipline*. Bill Isaacs, a young protégé of Bohm's, began the MIT Dialogue Project and took the practice into big companies. Today it is practiced widely, and the practice is spreading. Isaacs has said, "We can think of companies as networks of power or hierarchy or we can think of them as networks of conversation. Dialogue can change companies."

The Dialogue Group

In group psychology and in the corporate world, dialogue is practiced in what are called dialogue groups. There are also dialogue groups being run in schools, prisons, and local government offices. I personally have run them with companies, schools, and local politicians.

In the dialogue group, people sit in a circle to emphasize the absence of hierarchy. The ideal group size ranges from seven to twenty, so that everyone has a chance to participate fully. There should be no observers in a dialogue group, no fence-sitters. But one or two members of the circle act as facilitators. They participate fully, they are members of the group, but they also have the job of holding the group's energy, of maintaining a spirit of inquiry in the conversation, and if there is a theme, of gently ensuring that the conversation sticks to it more or less. The only real rules in dialogue are that each group member should express openly and honestly what he or she thinks or feels and that no one should be abusive. If the dialogue becomes too cerebral, if there is abuse, or if the conversation collapses into debate, the facilitator gently brings it back on track.

There is an assumption that the dialogue group is a sacred space. If people are to be honest and open, they have to feel safe. Comments should not go beyond the group. There should be no comeback for expressing unpopular ideas or for surfacing criticism. No one should fear sounding the fool. The facilitator has to build what Bill Isaacs calls "the container"—the space where dialogue can happen freely.

The dialogue group enables group feeling and group intelligence to emerge. As in quantum physics, the whole (the group) is larger than the sum of its parts (its individual members and their thoughts and feelings). This is why it can be a powerful process for organizational learning. It gives the corporation access to the corporate brain. During the dialogue itself, that corporate brain is almost tangibly present in the center of the circle. Bill Isaacs describes this tangible presence as a "field," the field of inquiry, the field of shared intelligence. It is very like the quantum field, the vacuum, out of which all things emerge. Dialogue is always full of surprises.

Dialogue group practitioners differ (as they should!) about the nature of the dialogue conversation. Some, following the tradition of Chris Argyris and "Action Science," think that the conversation should be goal directed, aimed at solving some specific problem. Critics say this is too mechanistic. Others prefer a completely open and nondirected conversation, letting whatever comes to mind emerge. Personally, I usually use a both-and approach, setting some vague theme but letting the conversation run widely.

Nondirected conversation is alien to companies, and many corporate people feel uncomfortable with nondirected dialogue. Some have got round this by having a group within the group. The dialogue group meets weekly or biweekly for at least six months, allowing itself a wide range of free-flowing inquiry. A subgroup within the dialogue group then meets separately to discuss how insights that emerge in the dialogue might be implemented for practical use.

The Dialogic Attitude

Dialogue groups are powerful vehicles for deep organizational transformation. They are a way of evoking and embedding quantum thinking, and thus form a useful "quantum infrastructure." But I think that dialogue is more than just a new kind of group conversation.

To me, dialogue is essentially an *attitude*. It is a radically different attitude toward oneself, toward others, toward knowledge and problems and relationships. It is new paradigm, quantum thinking in practice. If, deep inside ourselves and in our approach to others, we replaced knowing with finding out, answers with questions, winning or losing with sharing, inequality with equality, power with respect and reverence, and proving points with exploring possibilities and listening, then I think we really could change ourselves and our world. There would certainly be a different approach to work, innovation, challenge, and relationship in corporations.

Dialogue can be with a group, but it can also be internal. Each of us has many simultaneous conversations going on in our heads, simultaneous and conflicting impulses and desires. Usually we repress most and follow one. "This is the true voice of the real me." But they are all voices of me. The quantum self, we have seen, is a whole chorus of conversations. Dialogue can allow me to listen to myself in a new way, a more accepting and more creative way. At the same time, it can teach me to listen to intimate associates and work colleagues in a new way. It can teach me to hear the possibilities inside myself, inside others, and inside situations.

The Concept Cafe

The *concept cafe* is another form of gentle dialogue that a partner (Dr. Lilly Evans) and I have been using with corporate people. I referred to it earlier. It was first conceived as a "philosophers' supper" by Peter Isaac of Peter Chadwick Ltd. In its most simple terms, it is a Socratic dinner party, a modern, corporate symposium supper.

Businesspeople in particular are unused to sharing much of their private feelings and reflections with colleagues. Yet, as we have seen, it is these private dimensions of the self that possess so much of our energy and creativity, so much of our passion. The concept cafe is an indirect way of bringing people out by giving them someone else's sensitive reflections on which to comment. In our most popular concept cafe, we take readings from the great poems and essays of writers and thinkers who have shaped the thinking and feeling of the modern era. We call it "Voices of the Twentieth Century." It includes excerpts from the poems of people like William Butler Yeats, T.S. Eliot, and Rabindranath Tagore; from the songs of Bob Dylan and John Lennon; from the psychological writings of Sigmund Freud and Carl Jung; from the philosophy of Nietzsche and Martin

Buber; from the writings of the architect Le Corbusier; and from the business reflections of George Soros, Bill Gates, or Richard Branson.

Each person at the roundtable supper (maximum eleven per table) takes a quote from some famous voice, interprets it, and shares some personal reflections on it. Then others join in. People enjoy a good meal, enjoy good conversation about meaty issues they might not otherwise ever raise at a dinner party, and broaden their general knowledge. They also share aspects of themselves they have never shared with colleagues before. Afterward, most comment that they work together more closely and with greater mutual understanding. They see their business problems in a larger context.

9

Servant Leaders:

What Do They Really Serve?

Oh, this is the animal that never was.
They did not know it and, for all of that,
they loved his neck and posture, and his gait,
clean to the great eyes with their tranquil gaze.
Really it was not. Of their love they made it,
this pure creature. And they left a space
always, till in this clear uncluttered place
lightly he raised his head and scarcely needed
to be. They did not feed him any corn,
only the possibility he might
exist, which gave the beast such strength, he bore
a horn upon the forehead. Just one horn.
Unto a virgin he appeared, all white,
and was in the silver mirror and in her.

—Rainer Maria Rilke,
Sonnets to Orpheus, "The Unicorn"

Rainer Maria Rilke is generally considered the most influential German poet of the twentieth century. His work has caught and reflected some of the century's major concerns. This poem about the unicorn is one of the central readings in the concept cafe that my colleague and I run for business leaders. I think that it adds important new dimensions to discussions of the servant leader concept. More than that, I think these are particularly quantum dimensions, and that the servant leader concept is vital to understanding quantum leadership.

As I understand the term, servant leadership involves practicing the essence of quantum thinking. Servant leaders lead from that level of deep, revolutionary vision that is accessed only by the third of our three kinds of thinking. They change the system, invent the new paradigm, clear a space where something new can be. They accomplish this not just from "doing," but more fundamentally, from "being." All this makes servant leadership the essence of what this book is about. Such leaders are essential to deep corporate transformation. For this reason, I have chosen servant leadership as the book's final and summary theme.

> Servant leadership is the essence of quantum thinking
> and quantum leadership.

The unicorn has always been a special symbol in our culture. He is that most impossible creature of the human imagination, a beast conjured up by longing and the human capacity to dream. In Rilke's poem he is conjured up by love, and given a space to be by those who dare to believe in the possibility that he might exist. In quantum science, the whole of existence is a set of possibilities plucked out of the quantum vacuum's infinite sea of potentiality. Some of these possibilities are plucked out by observers, by human beings living our lives. An awareness of our role as cocreators of existence can increase our capacity to fulfill that role. Each of us is a servant of the vacuum, a servant of the manifold potentiality at the heart of existence.

Business leaders who become aware of servanthood in this sense know that they serve more than company or colleagues, more than markets or products, more even than vision and values as these are normally understood. They serve that longing that conjures up unicorns, and through this service they build or contribute to a successful—a profitable—business that adds some new dimension both to business and to human well-being.

One independent company founder with whom I spoke told me she could see three reasons why people might start up a business. The first reason is opportunity. The would-be entrepreneur looks at the market and sees that there is an opening for some service or product, and says, "Someone needs to provide this. I *will*." The second reason is talent or opportunity. The would-be entrepreneur looks inward at personal resources and skills or outward at the local environment and says, "I *can* provide this." The third reason is more spiritual. The future entrepreneur doesn't begin by thinking about business or a career, but about a feeling of inner necessity. "This *has to* exist. This *has* to happen. I *have* to do it." I think this is the beginning of the servant leader's business career.

There seems to me an interesting and useful interplay between these three motives for going into business, the three kinds of thinking our brains can do, and the three models of self and organization that we have looked at. The opportunity motive is very logical. I analyze the market, I see what is missing, I decide to provide it. This is the way my rule-bound, goal-oriented serial thinking operates. It's compatible with seeing myself as a Newtonian billiard ball in human form, as able to place myself in the scheme of things through manipulating and controlling the forces and bodies around me. It is management by objectives.

The skill motive is very associative. I am this sort of person with these sorts of resources, so I can see that I fit in here. This is the way the brain's parallel, networked thinking operates. Those things are most natural (those neural connections strongest) that conform to past experience, to habit, to the relationships around me. This is compatible with seeing myself in terms of my relationships to others, to what I can offer them. I find my place in some existing network. I go into the family craft or the family business. I deal locally, with familiar things and familiar people.

The inner necessity, "I *have* to" motive is quantum. The existing provisions, products, services, and so on are not adequate. Something new is needed here and I have to provide it. This is the way the brain's creative, rule-breaking, rule-making kind of thinking operates. Experience throws up things and events for which there are no previous neural connections, therefore no concepts or categories. So the brain creates new ones. It rewires itself. This is compatible with the quantum model of self where I see myself as a cocreator, as an active agent in this universe who makes things happen. If I want the world to change, I have to change it. If this product or service should exist, I have to provide it.

We've seen that in both the brain and in life's experiences, one reason why quantum thinking kicks in is that there is a crisis. We have little motive to change our neural wiring or our paradigm if the existing one is doing its job. Such crisis is common in the shift from normal or conservative science to revolutionary science. It often plays a role in the making of servant leaders. In their case this is often a spiritual crisis, some threat to their usual self-esteem, to their usual framework of meaning and value, some longing for something more.

Real Servant Leaders at Work

I have had the good fortune to know three such leaders personally and to know a bit about their stories. I want to share brief episodes from each because they throw light on those deeper dimensions of servant leadership that I think are associated with the vision of the new science.

JULIETTE'S STORY

This is a true story, but the names have been changed at the request of its subject. The leader I will call Juliette Johnson owns a small but growing business, "Juliette's Fashion Studios." The founding studio is located in Southeast England. She is in her early forties, a French immigrant to the United Kingdom who is married to an Englishman. It was Juliette who outlined the three reasons why someone might start up a business.

In France, Juliette was an opera star. She is a large woman with the broad chest and wide neck that are usually associated with a successful singing career, and she was successful. She had her success, a husband, two teenaged children, and a wide circle of friends. She dabbled in spiritual quest, but not seriously. Then, within the space of a year, her husband left her, her children decided to join their father, and her friends became critical and distant. "I was devastated," she says. "I didn't know what had happened. I didn't know where to turn."

On the advice of associates in England, Juliette signed up for a six-month extensive study course at a spiritual community in Scotland. She studied the writings of an eleventh-century Sufi mystic, Ibn Al'arabi, and those of ancient Eastern and more modern Western mystics, all of whom used their work to celebrate the unity of existence. Life at the community was quiet, disciplined, and reflective. Juliette was thrown back on herself and on a quest to discover what really mattered to her. During the course she met her future husband, an Englishman, and they moved on to the south of England.

Living in a small flat above a shop and supported through state welfare funds, Juliette had no clear sense of career direction. Then a friend asked her to help with a handmade dress. She had done sewing ever since her early teens, and the dress she now made for her friend awakened something. She made a few others and felt that in her original designs she saw an expression of the passion she had felt during her study course in Scotland, a passion to celebrate the unity of existence and the true reality that lies behind the human form. She felt that she *had* to make more dresses, whether or not anyone wanted to buy them. But people did buy them. Her designs were fresh; they brought out some special, deeply feminine quality in any woman who wore them. She consciously designed in a way that made bodily shape and size unimportant. "All bodies are beautiful," she says. "Every woman should be able to feel good about her body. She should feel happy about herself."

In fact, Juliette's clothes flatter something beyond the body, something even beyond the feminine. She smiles and says, "Yes, of course. It's a celebration of that source from which all form arises." The passion and the vision it inspired led to more designs, to the opening of a large shop, to the growth of a promising business. "It *had* to be a business," she says. "I had to show that I could serve something sacred *and* that I could do this inside a business. I wanted my business to be an act of service." Nonetheless, she is loath to describe herself as a servant leader. It seems too grand, too lacking in humility. Quoting the mystic who inspired her, she says, "Just say what you know. Don't say how you got there."

ANDREW STONE'S STORY

We've met Andrew Stone and his quantum leadership practices throughout this book. But there is a story behind Stone's career, a crisis that inspired his life and his work.

Andrew Stone is extremely well read, but he has little formal education. As he puts it, he left school "in disgrace" at age fifteen with only five "O" level exams, one of which was in woodwork. He began to live by his wits, as they say in England, and by the age of seventeen was a spiv in the street markets of Cardiff in Wales. A spiv is a seller of "dubious" goods. He had his own market stall where he could offer these wares, and he made a good living from it. "I had a car, a flat, and some good mates who, admittedly, were in the criminal world. I could pull any bird I wanted. I thought I was a very big deal."

Stone is from a Jewish family, though that had meant little to him. Still, in 1967, when the Six Days War broke out and friends chided him that if he was really such a big deal, he would go to Israel and fight, he went. As so many of us of that generation found, the war was over by the time he got there, but he decided to stay on for a while. But Israeli life didn't live up to his expectations. Or at least he felt his own life didn't live up to Israeli standards.

"I was used to pulling birds with a flashy car and fast line and a big wad of pound notes," he says. "Israeli girls could not have cared less. They wanted philosophical conversations about Jewish destiny and the meaning of life. They were attracted to war heroes and guys who wanted to dedicate themselves to something. I felt like shit. I felt I was a total nothing, a germ that ought to be eradicated." He spent a year in Israel feeling this way until he suddenly felt that he *had* to be of service. He couldn't justify living otherwise. "Even when I was a spiv," he says, "I wanted to make my customers happy. I always wanted to get them a good deal. Now I felt I had to play that out on a wider stage."

Stone wrote to his father, also a Jewish street trader back in Wales, about his new feelings, saying he wasn't sure how to act on them, what to do next. "My father reminded me of my skills at retailing and told me about the principles of Marks & Spencer, an idealist Jewish firm with a vision of serving the community. He said it was rare to combine in one person an intense belief in caring principles and knowledge of how to buy and sell profitably. There are do-gooders who can write and talk. There are traders who can turn a profit. But a great challenge would be to work for Marks & Spencer and try to carry on to the next generation this combination of great retailing done in a socially responsible way. I was inspired by this."

Stone went back to England and applied for a job at Marks & Spencer (M&S). He took the standard recruitment test and failed on every point. The recruitment officer at that time was David Sieff, son of the then chairman, and today director of community affairs at M&S. Sieff told Stone that by any of the normal criteria, he was unemployable. But at the same time, M&S at that time was aware of the growing dangers of its size and a tendency to become bureaucratic and institutionalized. They wanted to retain the skills of the entrepreneur that had built the company. "I have an instinct about you," Sieff told Stone. "I'll try you out for a year." The rest is company history.

KATSUHIKO YAZAKI'S STORY

Katsuhiko Yazaki is a Japanese businessman in his early fifties. He owns a global mail-order company named *Felissimo* with offices in Japan, Europe, and North America. His story is told in his 1994 book, *The Path to Liang Zhi.*

As a very young man, Yazaki had inherited a "storeless business" from his father. Goods were sold door to door, by word of mouth, through the network. Over the years, he built this up to a successful mail-order business that left him very wealthy. By his mid-forties, he had everything that he thought he wanted: success, wealth, esteem in the community, a family. But something was missing. Some friends showed him a book about Zen and told him of a Master Kido Inoue who taught it.

Yazaki went to Master Inoue's monastery for a week of meditation. He found it difficult, at times painful, but liberating. "One moment" he says, "I felt as if I had found peace, another moment I felt like a prisoner of my delusions. I was astonished at the realization of what I had been calling 'me.' This was the first time I realized how many delusions were within myself. It was also the first time I realized how many delusions I had that were causing ups and downs in my daily life. Until this point, I had never confronted realities about myself so directly."

Yazaki emerged from his monastery cell after a week "to see the beauty of the world for the first time." He realized that he had been living his life in shadow and that the world itself was being damaged by human shadows. "Humans," he wrote, "by separating the world from the self, nature from humanity, and the self from others, trap themselves in delusions to protect the ego. They inevitably enter a frightening scenario of hypocrisy and self-righteousness."

After these insights, Yazaki rededicated his business life. He wanted to use his company to do something for the earth's environment and for future generations. He renamed the company *Felissimo,* which means "happiness" in Spanish and Italian, because his vision of the proper role of business became to increase the sum of human happiness. He formed his new concept of the "ultra store," a store that can "gather value over a wide area" by transcending the limits of geographical space and present time. He felt that he could help his customers to realize images of their future selves and to imagine more fulfilling future lifestyles by marketing his goods globally, thus expanding service and awareness at a more universal level. He attended the Rio Earth Summit Conference and dedicated himself and much of his money to saving the earth's environment. He started a foundation to study the needs of future generations and to back needed educational projects. "I believe," he says, "that these international activities flowed from the development of our business as an ultra store and from my rethinking as a business owner." He readily quotes one of his heroes, Kazuo Inamori (founder of the Kyocera Corporation), who said that what he had done as a business owner was "to continue to raise the level of my ideology every day."

The Concept of Servant Leadership

Western businesspeople who have been discussing the servant leader concept do mean by this a leader who has a sense of deeper values and a leadership style that involves conscious service to these values. But we don't always mean the same thing when we speak about values. The usual Western corporate values, at their best, speak of things like excellence, fulfilling one's potential and allowing space for others to do so, achievement, quality of products and services, commitment to never-ending growth. In the East, traditionally, deep values have centered around things like compassion, humility, gratitude, service to one's family and community, service to the ancestors or to the ground of Being itself. Traditionally, the East has emphasized cooperation and trust; the West, competition and control. A "good man" in the East has a quality of *being.* In the West, a "good man" is usually measured by his quality of *doing.*

Robert Greenleaf, who wrote the original paper on servant leadership, had something more Eastern in mind. Indeed, he used the example of a Nepalese Buddhist monk. And in his recent book, *Synchronicity,* Joe Jaworski emphasizes the importance of *being* before *doing* in corporate leadership. He uses dialogue practice extensively as a way of helping leaders access the level of being within themselves. Jaworski's own life was turned around during an interview with David Bohm about the thinking in the new science. I deeply believe the conceptual structure of this new science can give us a more solid underpinning for understanding the true meaning of the servant leader. And a deeper understanding of what that leader serves.

As someone trained in physics at MIT, I know well from my own educational background the role that science and the wider spirit of Newtonian mechanism have played in widening the gulf between values associated with doing and those associated with being. Newtonian science is preoccupied with objects, obsessed with analysis and measurement. It draws a sharp divide between spirit and matter, between man and nature. And it gives us a concern with the here and now, a view of truth as black or white, a preoccupation with achievement and progress as measured by doing and acquiring. These are not the values that have inspired the three leaders whose stories I have cited.

We have seen that the new science of this century has a very different philosophical and conceptual basis. Quantum science tells us that the world is all of a piece, holistic. We human beings are in and of nature, we help to make reality happen, we are free agents with a responsibility for cocreation. More than that, quantum science shows us that we are, in our essential physical and spiritual makeup, *extensions,* "excitations," of the underlying ground state of Being. As I put it earlier, a quantum view of the self shows us that we are "thoughts in the mind of God."

To qualify as servant leaders in the deepest sense, I think that leaders must have four essential qualities. They must have a deep sense of the interconnectedness of life and all its enterprises. They must have a sense of engagement and responsibility, a sense of "I *have* to." They must be aware that all human endeavor, including business, is a part of the larger and richer fabric of the whole universe. And perhaps most important of all, servant leaders must know what they ultimately serve. They must, with a sense of humility and gratitude, have a sense of the Source from which all values emerge.

Describing the unicorn, Rilke said, "Really it was not. Of their love they made it." The servant leader serves from a base of love. The three whose examples I quoted do so—not from some gooey, sentimental love of all humanity and wish to do good works, but out of a deep, abiding passion for and commitment to service. And that service itself is to something beyond the given. A wish to make women feel good about themselves inspired by the underlying nature of existence. A wish to make people happy inspired by the Jewish love of community. A wish to serve future generations inspired by a vision of the interconnectedness of existence.

To these servant leaders and others like them, the business of business no longer restricts itself to manipulating things and nature and people for profit. Rather, business becomes a spiritual vocation in the largest sense of that word. The brain's "spirit" (quantum thinking) integrates the abilities of the brain's "intellect" (serial thinking) and the brain's "heart" (parallel thinking). As such, it initiates and perpetuates the brain's necessary rewiring. I believe that it is only from such a basis of spiritual servant leadership that really deep transformation can come about in the corporate world. Without it, there can be no fundamental rewiring of the corporate brain.

Afterword

There are definitive moments in all our lives when we each have the possibility to undergo dramatic regeneration. This is as true for corporations as for individuals. My personal "rewiring" began quite unexpectedly during a two-day seminar Danah Zohar and a colleague (Dr. Lilly Evans) were running for our senior project leaders. Danah's use of new science to rethink business strategies helped me realize just how mechanistic my colleagues and I had been. Those two days marked the beginning of a turnaround that has put Peter Chadwick on an exciting new course.

As Europe's fastest growing consultancy company, we were primed for something new. Since our founding in the U.K. in 1987, and under the careful tutelage of CEO Ian Clarkson and Chairman Quentin Baer, Peter Chadwick has enjoyed compound growth and is working with many blue-chip multinationals. Yet despite our extremely successful record in implementation consultancy, the challenge laid before us during those two days we worked with Danah and her colleague led us to undertake a journey to "rewire our corporate brain."

Adopting some of the leading-edge thinking, we restructured ourselves into a collection of self-organizing networks. Each network in turn focused on key issues, whether these were market, sector, or lateral learning opportunities that could benefit both ourselves and our clients. At the same time, we repositioned ourselves in the marketplace. It became our trademark to promote what at first seemed a very anticonsultant message: "For change to be sustainable, it must ultimately come from within."

The new science was a crucial element in changing our company thinking. But three other key elements we gained from that first two-day seminar with Danah and Lilly were the power of creative dialogue, the experience of the concept cafe, and the direct impact of using these experiences with clients. We have continued to use repeated bookings of that seminar to train all our staff, and now regularly offer it to clients. We have also formed the Peter Chadwick Leadership Institute to further develop these and other new approaches, and we are pleased to welcome Danah Zohar as a founding fellow.

Implementing the ideas found in *Rewiring the Corporate Brain* has made a significant difference to the self-understanding and practice of Peter Chadwick. I feel certain the book will enjoy a permanent place, not only on the corporate bookshelf, but more importantly in the spirit and soul of tomorrow's successful leaders.

—*Peter Isaac*
Director, Training and Development,
Peter Chadwick Ltd.

Bibliography

Argyris, Chris. "Good Communication That Blocks Learning." *Harvard Business Review* (July-August 1994).

Bohm, David, and F. David Peat. *Science, Order and Creativity.* New York: Bantam Books, 1987.

Carse, James. *Finite and Infinite Games.* New York: Ballantine Books, 1986.

Fei, Xiaotong. *From the Soil.* Berkeley: University of California Press, 1992.

Greenleaf, Robert. *Servant Leadership: A Journey into the Nature of Legitimate Power and Greatness.* New York: Paulist Press, 1977.

Hobbes, Thomas. *Leviathan.* Glasgow: William Collins, 1962.

Hobsbawm, Eric. *The Age of Extremes.* London: Michale Joseph, 1994.

Isaacs, William. "Dialogue." In *The Fifth Discipline Fieldbook,* edited by Peter Senge et al., 357-364. London: Nicholas Brealey, 1994.

Jaworski, Joseph. *Synchronicity.* San Francisco: Berrett-Koehler, 1996.

Kaku, Michio. *Hyperspace.* Oxford: Oxford University Press, 1994.

Kuhn, Thomas. *The Structure of Scientific Revolutions.* Chicago: University of Chicago Press, 1970.

Locke, John. In *Social Contract, The* by Jean-Jacques Rousseau. London and New York: Oxford University Press, 1952.

McRae, Hamish. *The World in 2020.* London: Harper Collins, 1995.

Marshall, Ian. "Three Kinds of Thinking." In *Towards a Scientific Basis for Consciousness,* edited by S. Hammeroff et al. Cambridge Mass: MIT Press, 1996.

Maslow, Abraham. *Motivation and Personality.* New York: Harper & Row, 1970.

Micklethwait, John, and Adrian Wooldridge. *The Witch Doctors.* London: Heinemann, 1996.

Nietzsche, Friedrich. *Thus Spoke Zarathustra.* New York and London: Penguin, 1961.

O'Shaughnessy, Arthur William Edgar. "Ode." In *The Oxford Book of Victorian Verse*. Oxford: Clarendon Press, 1925.

Pascale, Richard Tanner, and Anthony G. Athos. *The Art of Japanese Management*. New York and London: Penguin Books, 1982.

Quinn, Daniel. *Ishmael*. New York: Bantam Books, 1992.

Rilke, Rainer Maria. "The Unicorn." In *Sonnets to Orpheus*. Berkeley: The University of California Press, 1960.

Rycroft, Charles. *A Critical Dictionary of Psychoanalysis*. London: Thomas Nelson, 1968.

Senge, Peter. *The Fifth Discipline*. New York: Doubleday, 1990.

Soros, George. *The Atlantic Monthly* (January 1997).

Toffler, Alvin, and Heidi Toffler. *Creating a New Civilization*. Atlanta: Turner Publishing, 1994.

Trompenaars, Fons. *Riding the Waves of Culture*. London: Nicholas Brealey, 1993.

Waldrop, M. Mitchell. "The Trillion Dollar Brain of Dee Hock," *Fast Company Magazine* (October/November 1996).

Yazaki, Katshuiko. *The Path to Liang Zhi*. Kyoto, Japan: Future Generations Alliance Foundation, 1994.

Zohar, Danah. *The Quantum Self*. New York: William Morrow Quill; London: Harper Collins, 1990.

Zohar, Danah, and Ian Marshall. *The Quantum Society*. New York: William Morrow Quill; London: Harper Collins, 1994.

Zohar, Danah, and Ian Marshall. *Who's Afraid of Schrödinger's Cat?* New York: William Morrow; London: Bloomsbury, 1997.

Index

INDEX

INDEX

About the Author

DANAH ZOHAR was born and educated in the United States. She received her Bachelor of Science degree in physics and philosophy from MIT. She then did postgraduate work in philosophy, psychology, theology, and law at Harvard University. She is the author of the best-selling *The Quantum Self* and *The Quantum Society,* books that extend the language and principles of quantum physics into a new understanding of human consciousness, psychology, and social organization.

Zohar teaches in the Leading Edge course at Oxford Brookes University and in the Oxford Strategic Leadership Program at Oxford University's Templeton College.

For the past several years, Zohar has been active in management education and consultancy. Companies to which she has made in-house presentations at the senior management level have included the Swedish Forestry Commission, Volvo, Astra Pharmaceutical, Philip Morris Tobacco, Marks & Spencer, Shell, British Telecom, Motorola, Philips, Norwich Union Financial Services, Skandia Insurance and Financial Services, McCann Erikson, and McKinsey. She is on the faculty of Shell U.K.'s "Challenges for Change" senior management training program and has addressed the leadership team leading Shell USA's transformation process for senior management. Zohar has an ongoing relationship with senior management at Motorola, where she lectures frequently. She is an associate member of Joseph Jaworski's Centre for Generative Leadership, and a founding fellow of the Peter Chadwick Leadership Institute.

Danah Zohar lectures widely throughout the world at conferences organized by such bodies as UNESCO, the European Cultural Foundation, the World Economic Forum, the International Federation of Training and Development Organizations, the World Business Academy, the Swedish National Parliament, Japan's Council for the Growth of Future Generations, and the Australian National Government. She has addressed members of the Swedish National Parliament and has worked with local government representatives and educators in several countries.

Danah Zohar currently lives in Oxford, England, with her husband and two children. Recently she co-authored with her husband, Ian Marshall, *Who's Afraid of Schrödinger's Cat?* Published by Bloomsbury (UK) and William Morrow (USA) in March 1997, it is a survey of the new ideas of twentieth century science.

Berrett-Koehler Publishers

Berrett-Koehler is an independent publisher of books, periodicals, and other publications at the leading edge of new thinking and innovative practice on work, business, management, leadership, stewardship, career development, human resources, entrepreneurship, and global sustainability.

Since the company's founding in 1992, we have been committed to supporting the movement toward a more enlightened world of work by publishing books, periodicals, and other publications that help us to integrate our values with our work and work lives, and to create more humane and effective organizations.

We have chosen to focus on the areas of work, business, and organizations, because these are central elements in many people's lives today. Furthermore, the work world is going through tumultuous changes, from the decline of job security to the rise of new structures for organizing people and work. We believe that change is needed at all levels—individual, organizational, community, and global—and our publications address each of these levels.

We seek to create new lenses for understanding organizations, to legitimize topics that people care deeply about but that current business orthodoxy censors or considers secondary to bottom-line concerns, and to uncover new meaning, means, and ends for our work and work lives.

See next page for other books from Berrett-Koehler Publishers

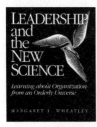
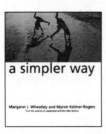
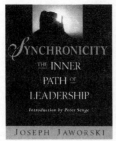